RICHARD III

By WILLIAM SHAKESPEARE

Preface and Annotations by
HENRY N. HUDSON

Introduction by
CHARLES HAROLD HERFORD

D1372570

Richard III
By William Shakespeare
Preface and Annotations by Henry N. Hudson
Introduction by Charles Harold Herford

Print ISBN 13: 978-1-4209-5462-3
eBook ISBN 13: 978-1-4209-5463-0

Cover Image: a detail of "David Garrick as Richard III", by William Hogarth, c. 1745, Walker Art Gallery, Liverpool, England.

Please visit *www.digireads.com*

CONTENTS

ACT V.

Introduction

Richard III., from the first one of the most popular plays of Shakespeare, was first printed, in Quarto, in 1597 under the title:

The Tragedy of | King Richard the third | Containing, | His treacherous Plots against his brother Clarence: | the pittiefull murther of his innocent nephewes: | his tyrannicall usurpation: with the whole course | of his detested life, and most deserved death. | As it has been lately Acted by the | Right honourable the Lord Chamber|laine his servants. AT LONDON | Printed by Valentine Sims, for Andrew Wise, | dwelling in Paules Churchyard, at the I Sign of the Angell. | 1597.

Seven other Quarto editions followed, in 1598, 1602, 1605, 1612, 1622, 1629, 1634, each apparently printed from its immediate predecessor, except that the Quarto of 1612 was printed from that of 1602. All seven, moreover, contained the name of Shakespeare on the title-page. In the interval between the sixth and seventh Quarto appeared the first Folio edition of the entire works. The title of the play here runs:

The Tragedie of Richard the Third: with the landing of Earle Richmond, and the Battell at Bosworth Field.

The text of the other three Folios is substantially identical with that of the first. On the other hand, the text of the first diverges widely from that of all the Quartos, and the divergence is of so complicated a kind that the determination of the relationship and authority of the two texts is one of the most serious enigmas of Shakespearean criticism.

The unquestioned facts are as follows:

1. The Quarto text (called here Q) contains thirty-two lines not found in the Folio (here called F);[1] F, on the other hand, contains about 200 lines not found in Q.[2] Nearly all these lines, both in Q and F, are clearly genuine.

2. Where the matter substantially corresponds, Q is frequently briefer in expression, less regular in grammar, style, metre, and punctuation; the stage directions are curter, and the dramatic machinery, here and there, simpler—*e.g.* Catesby superintends the execution of Hastings instead of Ratcliff and Lovel, while Surrey, who speaks a line in v. 1. 3 (F), has no part whatever in Q. But the brevity of Q is not seldom more forcible than the regularity of F.

3. Apart from these differences, the two texts show hundreds of

---

[1] The most important of these are: i. 3. 114; 4. 115-7, 137, 195, 243; ii. 2. 84-5, iii. 7. 220; iv. 2. 109-119; v. 3. 204-6.

[2] These are: i. 2. 16, 25, 115-167; 3. 116, 167-9; 4. 36, 37, 69-72, 115-6, 222, 266-9, 273, 275; ii. 1. 67; 2. 89-100, 123-140; iii. 1. 172-4; 3. 7, 8, 15; 4. 104-7; 5. 7, 103-5; 7. 5, 6, 37, 98-9, 120, 127, 144-53, 202, 245; iv. 1. 2-6, 37, 98-104; 4. 20-1, 28, 32, 53, 103, 159, 172, 179, 221-34, 276-7, 288-342, 400; v. 3. 27-8, 43.

slight variations for which no clear ground can be given.

Neither Q nor F thenceforth can claim to be exclusively Shakespeare's work, as regards at least the passages found in each alone. But the variations are sufficiently ambiguous to permit a good case to be made out for the decided superiority of either.

The extremer partisans of the Quarto (*e.g.* Mr. Gregory Foster) believe Q to represent Shakespeare's first draft, revised and compressed by himself, F the same draft edited and elaborated by another. The extremer partisans of the Folio (*e.g.* Delius,[3] Spedding,[4] Daniel[5]) regard Q as a more or less mutilated version of Shakespeare's work which F represents either in its original form (Delius) or after a revision by Shakespeare's own hand (Spedding). Mr. Daniel (in his Facsimile Reprint of Q_1) thinks that F represents the authentic theatrical text in use in 1623, the recent Quarto of 1622 being corrected for the press from it.

Neither of these extreme views seems quite adequate to the complexity of the facts. In both texts much must be allowed for mere blundering and carelessness; but it hardly admits of doubt that when we have removed this outer crust from Q_1 we get at work Shakespearean so far as it goes; when we have removed it from F we get at work which retains more of Shakespeare's material in a less purely Shakespearean form. When a play could remain for twenty-five years in the repertory of the company, a stage tradition inevitably grew up uncontrolled by the published texts. It is likely enough that Shakespeare himself contributed to this traditional version by alterations in his own text. But it is quite certain also that much more was contributed by some hand other than his, probably after his retirement and without his concurrence. This editor may have independently emended, or he may simply have recorded changes long established in stage tradition. The ideal aim, then, of the modern editor must be to detect and eliminate the work of both kinds done by this ancient editor upon Shakespeare's original or revised draft. Since, however, both the original draft and the extent of Shakespeare's revision are unknown, these sources of corruption can be certainly detected only in a minimum of cases. Hence the Cambridge editors adopted, as a *pis aller*, the practical alternative of substituting in doubtful cases the reading of Q, freed from mere blunders, for that of F; properly preferring the risk of excluding Shakespeare's final touches to that of including those of a hand not his at all.

---

[3] *Jahrbuch der deutschen Shakespeare Gesellschaft*, Bd. vii.
[4] *New Shakspere Society Transactions*, 1875-6.
[5] Facsimile Reprint of Q_1.

The chief characteristics of the editor seem to be as follows:

1. He *modernises.* Hence certain phrases and usages in Q, familiar to Shakespeare elsewhere, are replaced by others which had become more current in the second decade of the seventeenth century. Thus *which* is often changed to *that, betwixt* to *between, moe* to *more.*

2. He *regulates.*

(*a*) *metre.* He dislikes half-lines and long lines: *e.g.* iii. 4. 10-12 (in reply to Ely's 'Your grace, we think, should soonest know his mind' Q has:

> *Buck.* Who, I, my lord? we know each other's faces,
> But for our hearts, he knows no more of mine
> Than I of yours;
> Nor I no more of his than you of mine.

F:

> We know each other's faces; for our hearts,
> He knows no more of mine, than I of yours;
> Nor I of his, my lord, than you of mine.[6]

In iii. 5. 108 he even sacrifices a modern phrase for metrical regularity:

Q:

> And to give notice that no manner of person,

F:

> And to give notice that no manner person—

an archaism unknown to Shakespeare.

(b) *style.* He avoids repetitions of the same word even where this is stylistically right; *e.g.* i. 4. 18. Q:

> Methought that Gloster stumbled; and, in stumbling,
> Struck me, that thought to stay him, overboard.

---

[6] Similar regulations of metre are particularly obvious in the following lines, among others, i. 1. 75 (F_1 *was, for her*).

F:

> . . . and in *falling.*

So, in i. 2. 76, he substitutes *crimes* for *evils,* apparently to avoid its recurrence in v. 79, notwithstanding that the repetition has point.

3. He *emends feebly.*

In iv. 4. 41 (Margaret's enumeration of her losses) Q had, by a slip:

> I had a *Richard* till a Richard kill'd him.

F corrects:

> I had a *husband,* etc.

whereas the series of proper names in the context demand the proper name here. Capell first proposed 'Henry.'

In iii. 7. 219, Buckingham concludes his feigned appeal to Richard with Q:

> Come citizens; zounds! I'll entreat no more:

And Richard piously rejoins:

> O do not swear, my lord of Buckingham!

Before the date of the Folio, the statute against oaths had no doubt necessitated an alteration of the passage: but it was a poor refuge to excise this lively trait altogether, as in F where Buckingham's speech ends with the tame

Come, citizens, we will entreat no more.

In iv. 4. 129 a just though somewhat difficult expression is emended into nonsense. Elizabeth is pleading for the free expression of their grief in words.

Q:

> Windy attorneys to their client woes,
> Airy succeeders of *intestate* joys, . . .
> Let them have scope; tho' what they do impart
> Help nothing else, yet do they ease the heart.

F, apparently connecting the joys which the words 'succeed' with the 'heart' which they 'ease,' substitutes *intestine* for *intestate.*

Notwithstanding the delinquencies of the editors, the Folio text is, however, in a number of passages clearly superior in authority to Q; whether through retaining Shakespeare's original draft or having enjoyed his subsequent revision, cannot always be determined. Thus in iv. 1. 26-27, Brakenbury's refusal of admission to the Duchess reads in Q:

> I do beseech your graces all to pardon me;
> I am bound by oath, I may not do it.

In F:

> No, madam, no, I may not leave it so:
> I am bound by oath, and therefore pardon me.

In iii. 6. 12, where Q has:

> Why, who's so gross
> That sees not this palpable device,
> Yet who's so blind, but says he sees it not?

F rightly gives *bold* for *blind.*

In the present text the readings of F have been rather more freely adopted than they were by the Camb. edd.

Beyond the publication of the first Quarto in 1597, no definite evidence of the date of *Richard III.* exists. But it had certainly been on the stage for at least three years, and several convergent reasons lead to the conclusion that it was written in 1593-4. (1) In 1594 was published an old play on the same subject, *The True Tragedie of Richard the third*[7] . . . 'as it was played by the Queenes Majesties Players.' The brilliant stage success of Shakespeare's *Richard* (with Burbage as the king[8]) probably induced the publication of this infantine production. (2) *Richard III.* is, in Shakespeare's treatment, the indispensable last act of the drama exhibited in the three Parts of *Henry VI*, and was beyond question written while his work upon these was still fresh. The First Part was a new play in 1591 and already famous, as has been seen, in 1592; the Second and Third Parts had provoked Greene's bitter taunt

---

[7] Reprinted by the Shakespeare Society in 1844.

[8] Burbage shortly became identified with the part. Cf.—in addition to a well-known anecdote—the lines of Richard Corbet, *c.* 1620, in his *Iter Boreale*, on the host 'full of ale and history,' who besides knowing the very spot on Bosworth field 'where Richmond stood, where Richard fell,' showed likewise authentic knowledge of the play:

> For when he would have sayd, King Richard dyed,
> And call's A horse! A horse!—he Burbidge cry'de.

Cent Sh. Pr. p. 128.

towards the close of the same year. (3) Shakespeare wrote *Richard III.*—alone of all the plays in which he was undoubtedly sole author—under the fascination of Marlowe's great but alien genius. That spell he had already put by when he wrote *Richard II.* not later than 1594, still more when he wrote *The Merchant of Venice* in 1595-6. Marlowe's scornful rejection of the jigging vein of rhyming mother wits is responsible for the exclusive use of blank verse. The high-strung intensity of tone, which continually gives a lyric afflatus to his dramatic dialogue, has found an echo in the choric lamentations of the bereaved women (ii. 2., iv. 1.). But above all, Marlowe has influenced his treatment of the story itself.

The story of Richard had obvious attractions for a Tudor dramatist, and at least two plays upon it were extant when Shakespeare wrote his own. To the *True Tragedie*, already mentioned, he possibly owed the suggestion of a phrase or two ('A horse, a horse, a fresh horse'); the Latin play *Ricardus Tertius*, by R. Legge, acted at Cambridge before 1583, he probably never saw. The basis of his own *Richard*, as of his other *Histories*, was the *Chronicle* of Holinshed occasionally supplemented by that of Halle. These materials, however, he handled with a genial and masterful audacity hardly matched elsewhere.

Holinshed's narrative of the two reigns of Edward IV. and Richard was derived, as has been seen, from two authorities very differently disposed towards the usurper. His Richard accordingly passes somewhat suddenly from a ruthless but loyal champion of the house of York to the consummate egoist, drawn in the vindictive *Life* by More, 'I am myself alone.' Shakespeare throws the shadow of More's King Richard back upon the Duke of Gloster. Hence, while the Shakespearean Richard is plainly recognisable in Holinshed's, his colossal figure is defined with a far more peremptory emphasis: one motive shapes his whole life. Shakespeare's boldest changes are naturally in the first and second acts, preceding Edward's death. He does not attribute any action to Gloster of which Holinshed did not report that he had been suspected; but he is suspected of nothing which Shakespeare does not attribute to him.

Thus the marriage of Richard with Prince Edward's widow, recorded by Holinshed without remark, becomes in Shakespeare's version a master-stroke of cynical effrontery, carried out in circumstances studiously calculated to exhibit at their utmost height, not his statecraft, for his hinted politic reasons for the marriage remain wholly obscure, but his prodigious energy of will and intellect, his Macchiavellian *virtù*.[9] The scene does not advance the action, *i.e.* the career of Richard, in the least; its only outcome is to provide him with another obstacle to be removed; but it contributes wonderful touches to

---

[9] It may well have been suggested by Tamburlane's masterful wooing of Zenocrate.

Richard's portrait, and the weak hapless Anne, wedded only to be 'found worthy of death' is not the least pathetic of his victims.

The death of Clarence, again, was, according to Holinshed's cautious narrative, 'by some wise men' attributed to Gloster's covert influence over the king. Popular rumour attributed it to 'a foolish prophesie which was that, after King Edward, one should reigne, whose first letter of his name should be a G.' Shakespeare makes Gloster himself invent and publish the prophecy, and give practical effect to his own covert counsel by quietly procuring the murder. Holinshed's Richard is as malignant and as resolute, but he is more cautious, and he has reason to be so. For he has to deceive or to master the trained political intelligence of England. For Shakespeare's Richard this obstacle is insignificant, for of that political intelligence there is very little to be seen. The 'Citizens' who in ii. 3. timidly shake their heads as they 'see the waters swell before a boisterous storm,' but 'leave it all to God' are not men before whom very great circumspection was needed. Gloster might publish his prophecy among them without great risk of their applying it to his own name, as we know that the people actually did. And they are fitly represented by the credulous Mayor of iii. 5. In Holinshed this farcical scene is a farce on both sides. Richard, immediately after the dinner which he would not eat till Hastings was dead, 'sent in all hast for manie substantiall men out of the citie unto the Towre' and tells his story of treason suddenly discovered and promptly suppressed. 'And this he required them to report.' Whereupon 'everie man answered him faire, as though no man mistrusted the matter, which in truth no man beleeved' (Hoi. iii. 723; Stone, p. 374). Even Buckingham was not, in the opinion of the wisest contemporary judges, as reported by Holinshed, taken fully into Richard's counsel until the princes were safely in the Tower; whereas the Shakespearean Richard has frankly confided his purpose while still on their way to London, and is aided by his cunning connivance (Stone, p. 361).

Shakespeare's Richard is certainly Marlowesque in conception and execution. Marlowe's influence is visible in his colossal singleness of make, his transparent hypocrisy. His motives are as unmixed as Tamburlane's, and as frankly disclosed. But the moral atmosphere in which he is set is not altogether of Marlowe. Shakespeare's profounder ethical instinct, his more imaginative discernment of the issues of good and evil, is already apparent in the blending of the classical conception of Nemesis with the Marlowesque idealisation of Force. Innocent and guilty go down with no whisper of resistance before Richard; but his strokes are the instrument of the Nemesis invoked by Margaret's curse. Over against Richard the Titan stands Margaret the Fate; in her presence alone his genius is cowed, his 'angel becomes a fear, as being overpower'd.' The fear, silent by day, grows lurid nightly in evil dreams, which culminate in the spectral horrors of the eve of Bosworth.

His victims themselves grow clear-sighted in their last moments and recognise the web of guilt and retribution in which they are involved.

> Now Margaret's curse is fall'n upon our heads,
> For standing by when Richard stabb'd her son.
> Then cursed she Hastings, then cursed she Buckingham,
> Then cursed she Richard. O, remember, God,
> To hear her prayers for them, as now for us!
>
> (iii. 3. 15).

The significance of Margaret is heightened by the bold disregard for history and probability with which she is introduced. The real Margaret had been (after Tewkesbury, 1471) first imprisoned in the Tower, then ransomed by her father (1475), and had died in 1482.[10] Shakespeare makes her defy a decree of banishment and beard Richard with impunity before his own palace. More nearly than any other figure in the Histories, she moves with supernatural exemption from the bonds of space and time, 'seems not like the inhabitants of earth, and yet is on 't.'

Richard III. and *Romeo and Juliet* were probably in 1594-5 Shakespeare's most famous plays. *Richard III.* among the purely historical plays has never lost this rank, for the unrivalled glory of Falstaff belongs to comedy. Already in 1595 John Weever addressed one of his *Epigrammes* (printed 1599) to 'Gulielmus Shakespeare,' in which he refers to 'Romeo, Richard, more whose names I know not' as famous characters.[11] 'A horse! a horse! my kingdom for a horse' seems to have at once caught the popular ear and passed into a proverb; it is repeatedly quoted and parodied by Marston.[12] The opening lines were parodied in *The Returne from Parnassus* (1601-2). The ghostly visitations of the eve of Bosworth were adapted to the history of an earlier tyrant in the Latin play *Fatum Vortigerni.*[13] In 1614 one Christopher Brooke published a curious poetic rhapsody, *The Ghost of Richard III., Expressing himselfe in these three parts,* 1. *His Character,* 2. *His Legend,* 3. *His Tragedie,* and eking out his stiff verses with a Shakespearean phrase or two. The rival company attempted to profit by the attractions of the subject; and Henslowe records two plays on the subject, one (unfortunately lost) by Ben Jonson—*Richard Crookback* (June 1602). It would have been highly interesting to see what the author of *Sejanus* and of *Volpone* made of Richard. Early in the eighteenth century *Richard* underwent an adaptation at the hands of

---

[10] Halle, 301 (Stone's *Holinshed*, p. 342).

[11] In the original *Romeo-Richard.*

[12] *Cent, of Sh.'s Praise,* pp. 29 f.

[13] Churchill and Keller, 'Die latein. Univ.dramen Englands in der Zeit der Kön. Elisabeth' (*Sh. JB.* xxxiv. 259).

Colley Cibber, which fatally curtailed its splendid exuberance, but remains the stage version to this day.

CHARLES H. HERFORD

1899.

Preface

Registered at the Stationers' in October, 1597, as "The Tragedy of King Richard the Third, with the Death of the Duke of Clarence," and published in quarto the same year, but without the author's name. In 1598 it was issued again, with "By William Shakespeare" added in the title-page. There was a third issue in 1602, which, though merely a reprint of the former, claimed to be "newly augmented." The same text was printed again in 1605, and also in 1613, besides three other editions in quarto, severally dated 1624, 1629, and 1634; in all, eight quarto editions. The play was also printed in the folio of 1623, with a few brief omissions, with considerable additions, amounting to some hundred and eighty lines, and with many slight variations of text. A report of these additions may have prompted the insertion of "newly augmented" in the quarto of 1602, the publisher wishing to have it thought that his copy included them.

The great popularity of the play is shown by these frequent issues, wherein it surpassed any other of the Poet's dramas; and the three later quartos prove that even after the issue of the folio there was still a large demand for it in a separate form. It was also honoured beyond any of its fellows by contemporary notice. It is mentioned by Meres in his *Wit's Commonwealth*, 1598; Fuller, also, in his *Church History*, and Milton, in one of his political eruptions, refer to it as well known; and Bishop Corbet, writing in 1617, gives a quaint description of his host at Bosworth, which is highly curious, as witnessing both what an impression the play had made on the popular mind, and also how thoroughly the hero had become identified with Richard Burbage, the original performer of that part:

> Why, he could tell
> The inch where Richmond stood, where Richard fell.
> Besides what of his knowledge he could say,
> He had authentic notice *from the play*;
> Which I might guess by's *mustering up the ghosts*,
> And policies not incident to hosts;
> But chiefly by that one perspicuous thing
> Where he mistook *a player for a king*.
> For, when he would have said, King Richard died,
> And call'd "A horse, a horse!" *he Burbage cried.*

As to the time of the writing, we have no clear external evidence beyond the forecited entry at the Stationers'. The internal evidence makes strongly for as early a date as 1592 or 1593. The general style, though showing a decided advance on that of the Second and Third Parts of *King Henry the Sixth*, is strictly continuous with it; while the history and characterization of the three so knit in together as to make them all of one piece and texture. In several passages of the play, especially in Clarence's account of his dream, and Tyrrell's description of the murder of the young Princes, Shakespeare is out in his plenitude of poetical wealth; and the character of Richard is a marvel of sustained vigour and versatile aptness: nevertheless the play, as a whole, evinces somewhat less maturity of power than *King Richard the Second*: in several cases there is great insubordination of details to the general plan; as in the hero's wooing of Lady Anne and Queen Elizabeth, where we have an excess of dialogical epigram, showing indeed a prodigious fertility of thought, but betraying withal a sort of mental incontinence; and where we quite miss that watchful judgment which, in the Poets later dramas, tempers all the parts and elements into artistic symmetry and proportion. Therewithal the play has great and manifest inequalities of workmanship, insomuch as well-nigh to force the conclusion that the Poet must have revised it after a considerable interval, and given it many touches of his riper and more practised hand.

Historically considered, the play covers a period of fourteen years, namely, from the death of Henry, in 1471, to the fall of Richard, in 1485. More than half of this period, however, is dispatched in the first Act; the funeral of Henry, the marriage of Richard with Lady Anne, and the death of Clarence being represented as occurring all about the same time; whereas in fact they were separated by considerable intervals, the latter not taking place till 1478. And there is a similar abridgment of time between the first Act and the second; as the latter opens with the sickness of King Edward, his seeming reconciliation of the peers, and his death, all which took place in April, 1483. Thenceforward the events are mainly disposed in the order of their actual occurrence; the drama being perhaps as true to the history as were practicable or desirable in a work so different in its nature and use.—This drawing together of the scattered events seems eminently judicious: for the plan of the drama required them to be used only as subservient to the hero's character; and it does not appear how the Poet could have ordered them better for developing in the most forcible manner his idea of that extraordinary man. So that the selection and grouping of the secondary incidents are regulated by the paramount law of the work; and, certainly, they are made to tell with masterly effect in furtherance of the author's purpose.

Since Shakespeare's time, much has been written to explode the current history of Richard, and to lessen, if not remove, the abhorrence in which his memory had come to be held. The Poet has not been left without his share of criticism and censure for the alleged blackening of his dramatic hero. This attempt at reforming public opinion was led off by Sir George Buck, whose *History of Richard the Third* was published in 1646. Something more than a century later, the work was resumed and carried on with great acuteness by Horace Walpole in his *Historic Doubts*. And several other writers have since put their hands to the same task. Still the old judgment seems likely to stand. Lingard has carried to the subject his usual candour and research, and. after dispatching the strong points on the other side, winds up his account of Richard thus: "Writers have indeed in modern times attempted to prove his innocence; but their arguments are rather ingenious than conclusive, and dwindle into groundless conjectures when Confronted with the evidence which may be arrayed against them." The killing of the two Princes formed the backbone of the guilt laid at Richard's door. That they did actually disappear is tolerably certain; that upon him fell whatever advantage could grow from their death is equally so; and it is for those who deny the cause uniformly assigned at the time and long after for their disappearance to tell us how and by whom they were put out of the way. And Sharon Turner, who is perhaps the severest of all sifters of historic fictions, is constrained to admit Richard's murder of his nephews; and, so long as this bloodstain remains, the scouring of others, however it may diminish his crimes, will hardly lighten his criminality.

As to the moral complexion of Shakespeare's Richard, the incidents whereby his character in this respect transpires are nearly all taken from the historians, with only such heightening as it is the prerogative of poetry to lend, even when most tied to actual events. In the Poets time, the prevailing ideas of Richard were derived from the history of his life and reign put forth by Sir Thomas More; though the matter is supposed to have been mainly furnished by Dr. John Morton, who was himself a part of the subject, and was afterwards Cardinal, Primate of England, and Lord Chancellor to Henry the Seventh. More's *History*, as it is called, was adopted by both Hall and Holinshed into their *Chronicles*. It is a very noble composition; and Shakespeare's Richard, morally speaking, is little else than the descriptive analysis there given reduced to dramatic life and expression.

I must add, that after the battle of Tewksbury, in May, 1471, Queen Margaret was in fact confined in the Tower till 1475, when she went into France, and died there in 1482. So that the part she takes in this play is a dramatic fiction. And a very judicious fiction it is too. Nor is it without a basis of truth; for, though absent in person, she was nevertheless present in spirit, and in the memory of her voice, which still seemed to be ringing in the ears of both friends and foes. And her curses do but proclaim those moral retributions of which God is the author, and Nature His minister; and perhaps the only way her former character could be carried on into these scenes, was by making her seek indemnity for *her* woes by ringing changes upon the woes of others.

HENRY N. HUDSON

1888.

RICHARD III

Dramatis Personae.

EDWARD THE FOURTH
EDWARD, *Prince of Wales, his Son.*
RICHARD, *Duke of York, his Son.*
Duke of Clarence, *his Brother.*
Duke of Gloucester, *his Brother.*
A young son of Clarence.
HENRY TUDOR, *Earl of Richmond.*
BOURCHIER, *Primate of England.*
ROTHERHAM, *Archbishop of York.*
JOHN MORTON, *Bishop of Ely.*
STAFFORD, *Duke of Buckingham.*
JOHN HOWARD, *Duke of Norfolk.*
THOMAS, *his Son, Earl of Surrey.*
WOODVILLE, *Earl Rivers.*
Marquis of Dorset, *Son of the Queen.*
RICAHRD LORD GREY, *Son of the Queen.*
JOHN DE VERE, *Earl of Oxford.*
WILLIAM LORD HASTINGS.
THOMAS LORD STANLEY.
FRANCIS LORD LOVEL
SIR THOMAS VAUGHAN.
SIR RICHARD RATCLIFF.
SIR WILLIAM CATESBY.
SIR JAMES TYRREL.
SUR WILLIAM BRANDON.
SIR JAMES BLOUNT
SIR WALTER HERBERT
SIR ROBERT BRAKENBURY.
CHRISTOPHER URSWICK, *a Priest*
Another Priest.
Lord Mayor of London.
Sheriff of Wiltshire.
ELIZABETH, *Queen to King Edward IV*
MARGARET, *Widow of King Henry VI*
CECILY, *Duchess of York*
LADY ANNE.
A young Daughter of Clarence

Lords and other Attendants; two Gentlemen, a Pursuivant, Scrivener, Citizens, Murderers, Messengers, Ghosts, Soldiers, &c.

SCENE. *England.*

ACT I.

SCENE I.

London. A street.

[*Enter* GLOUCESTER.]

GLOUCESTER. Now is the winter of our discontent
    Made glorious Summer by this sun,[1] of York;
    And all the clouds that lour'd upon our house
    In the deep bosom of the ocean buried.
    Now are our brows bound with victorious wreaths;
    Our bruised arms hung up for monuments;
    Our stern alarums changed to merry meetings,
    Our dreadful marches to delightful measures.[2]
    Grim-visaged war hath smooth'd his wrinkled front;
    And now, instead of mounting barbed[3] steeds
    To fright the souls of fearful[4] adversaries,
    He capers nimbly in a lady's chamber
    To the lascivious pleasing of a lute.
    But I, that am not shaped for sportive tricks,
    Nor made to court an amorous looking-glass;
    I, that am rudely stamp'd, and want love's majesty
    To strut before a wanton ambling nymph;
    I, that am curtail'd of this fair proportion,[5]
    Cheated of feature by dissembling Nature,[6]
    Deformed, unfinish'd, sent before my time
    Into this breathing world, scarce half made up,

---

[1] The cognizance of Edward IV. was *a sun*, in memory of the three suns which are said to have appeared at the battle he gained over the Lancastrians at Mortimer's Cross.

[2] *Measure* was the name of a *dance.*

[3] *Barbed* is *caparisoned* or *clothed* in the trappings of war. The word is properly *barded*, from equus *bardatus.*

[4] *Fearful* was, as it still is, used in the two opposite senses of *terrible* and *timorous.* Here it probably has the former.

[5] *Proportion* for *form, shape*, or *personal aspect.* Repeatedly so. "This fair proportion" may refer to what has just been spoken of as "love's majesty." But *this* is probably here used indefinitely, and with something of a sneer. The demonstrative pronouns were, and still are, often used thus. So in *2 Henry IV.*, i. 2 : "*This* apoplexy is, as I take it, a kind of lethargy."

[6] *Feature* in the sense of *form* or *figure*, and referring to the person in general. So in More's description of Richard: "Little of stature, *ill-featured of limbs*, crook-backed."— *Dissembling*, here, is sometimes explained to mean, not *deceiving*, but putting together or *assembling* things not *semblable*, as a brave mind and a deformed body. It may be so; but the word *cheated* seems to make rather strongly against this explanation.

And that so lamely and unfashionable
That dogs bark at me as I halt by them;
Why, I, in this weak piping time of peace,
Have no delight to pass away the time,
Unless to spy my shadow in the sun
And descant on mine own deformity:
And therefore, since I cannot prove a lover,
To entertain these fair well-spoken days,
I am determined to prove a villain
And hate the idle pleasures of these days.
Plots have I laid, inductions[7] dangerous,
By drunken prophecies, libels and dreams,
To set my brother Clarence and the king
In deadly hate the one against the other:
And if King Edward be as true and just
As I am subtle, false and treacherous,
This day should Clarence closely be mew'd up,[8]
About a prophecy, which says that G
Of Edward's heirs the murderer shall be.
Dive, thoughts, down to my soul: here Clarence comes.—

[*Enter* CLARENCE, *guarded, and* BRAKENBURY.]

Brother, good day; what means this armed guard
That waits upon your grace?
CLARENCE. His majesty
Tendering[9] my person's safety, hath appointed
This conduct[10] to convey me to the Tower.
GLOUCESTER. Upon what cause?
CLARENCE. Because my name is George.
GLOUCESTER. Alack, my lord, that fault is none of yours;
He should, for that, commit your godfathers:
O, belike his majesty hath some intent
That you shall be new-christen'd in the Tower.
But what's the matter, Clarence? may I know?
CLARENCE. Yea, Richard, when I know; for I protest
As yet I do not: but, as I can learn,
He hearkens after prophecies and dreams;

---

[7] *Inductions* are beginnings, preparations; things that draw on or *induce* events. Shakespeare has the word just so in two other places.

[8] To *mew up* was a term in falconry; hawks being shut up or confined in a *mew* during the season of moulting.

[9] To *tender* a thing is to be *careful* of it, to have a *tender regard* for it, to *hold it dear*.

[10] *Conduct* for *conductor*, or *escort*.

And from the cross-row[11] plucks the letter G.
And says a wizard told him that by G
His issue disinherited should be;
And, for[12] my name of George begins with G,
It follows in his thought that I am he.
These, as I learn, and such like toys[13] as these
Have moved his highness to commit me now.
GLOUCESTER. Why, this it is, when men are ruled by women:
    'Tis not the king that sends you to the Tower:
    My Lady Grey his wife, Clarence, 'tis she
    That tempers[14] him to this extremity.
    Was it not she and that good man of worship,
    Anthony Woodeville,[15] her brother there,
    That made him send Lord Hastings to the Tower,
    From whence this present day he is deliver'd?
    We are not safe, Clarence; we are not safe.
CLARENCE. By heaven, I think there's no man is secure
    But the queen's kindred and night-walking heralds
    That trudge betwixt the king and Mistress Shore.
    Heard ye not what an humble suppliant
    Lord hastings was to her for his delivery?
GLOUCESTER. Humbly complaining to her deity
    Got my lord chamberlain his liberty.
    I'll tell you what; I think it is our way,
    If we will keep in favour with the king,
    To be her men and wear her livery:
    The jealous o'erworn widow and herself,[16]
    Since that our brother dubb'd them gentlewomen.
    Are mighty gossips in this monarchy.
BRAKENBURY. I beseech your graces both to pardon me;
    His majesty hath straitly given in charge
    That no man shall have private conference,
    Of what degree soever, with his brother.

---

[11] *Cross-row* is an abbreviation of *Christ-cross-row*, and means the *alphabet*, which is said to have been so called, either because a cross was placed before it, or because it was written in the form of a cross, to be used as a sort of charm.

[12] *For* is here equivalent to *because*; a frequent usage.

[13] *Toys* for *whims, fancies*, or *freaks of imagination*. So in Hamlet, i. 4: "The very place puts toys of desperation into every brain that looks so many fathoms to the sea," &c.

[14] *Tempers* is *frames, fashions*, or *disposes*.

[15] This name is here three syllables. Commonly spelt *Woodville*.

[16] The *widow* is Queen Elizabeth, the name of whose deceased husband was Grey. *Herself* refers to Mrs. Jane Shore, quite a noted character of the time, whom King Edward is said to have cherished as a sort of left-hand wife. She was much mixed up with the intrigues of the Court.

GLOUCESTER. Even so; an't please your worship, Brakenbury,
  You may partake of any thing we say:
  We speak no treason, man: we say the king
  Is wise and virtuous, and his noble queen
  Well struck in years, fair, and not jealous;
  We say that Shore's wife hath a pretty foot,
  A cherry lip, a bonny eye, a passing pleasing tongue;
  And that the queen's kindred are made gentle-folks:
  How say you sir? Can you deny all this?
BRAKENBURY. With this, my lord, myself have nought to do.
GLOUCESTER. Naught to do with mistress Shore! I tell thee, fellow,
  He that doth naught[17] with her, excepting one,
  Were best he do it secretly, alone.
BRAKENBURY. What one, my lord?
GLOUCESTER. Her husband, knave: wouldst thou betray me?
BRAKENBURY. I beseech your grace to pardon me, and withal
  Forbear your conference with the noble duke.
CLARENCE. We know thy charge, Brakenbury, and will obey.
GLOUCESTER. We are the Queen's abjects,[18] and must obey.
  Brother, farewell: I will unto the king;
  And whatsoever you will employ me in,
  Were it to call King Edward's widow sister,
  I will perform it to enfranchise you.
  Meantime, this deep disgrace in brotherhood
  Touches me deeper than you can imagine.
CLARENCE. I know it pleaseth neither of us well.
GLOUCESTER. Well, your imprisonment shall not be long;
  I will deliver you, or else lie for you:[19]
  Meantime, have patience.
CLARENCE. I must perforce. Farewell.

  [*Exeunt* CLARENCE, BRAKENBURY, *and Guard.*]

GLOUCESTER. Go, tread the path that thou shalt ne'er return.
  Simple, plain Clarence! I do love thee so,
  That I will shortly send thy soul to heaven,
  If heaven will take the present at our hands.
  But who comes here? the new-deliver'd Hastings?

---

[17] Richard is quibbling between *nought* and *naught*, the latter of which has the sense of *bad*, as in our word *naughty*.

[18] The lowest of her subjects. This substantive is found in Psalm xxxv. 15: "Yea, the very *abjects* came together against me unawares, making mouths at me, and ceased not."

[19] Or else *lie in prison* in your stead. But a quibble is probably intended between the two senses of *lie*.

[*Enter* HASTINGS.]

HASTINGS. Good time of day unto my gracious lord!
GLOUCESTER. As much unto my good lord chamberlain!
    Well are you welcome to the open air.
    How hath your lordship brook'd imprisonment?
HASTINGS. With patience, noble lord, as prisoners must:
    But I shall live, my lord, to give them thanks
    That were the cause of my imprisonment.
GLOUCESTER. No doubt, no doubt; and so shall Clarence too;
    For they that were your enemies are his,
    And have prevail'd as much on[20] him as you.
HASTINGS. More pity that the eagle should be mew'd,
    While kites and buzzards prey at liberty.
GLOUCESTER. What news abroad?
HASTINGS. No news so bad abroad as this at home;
    The King is sickly, weak and melancholy,
    And his physicians fear him[21] mightily.
GLOUCESTER. Now, by Saint Paul,[22] this news is bad indeed.
    O, he hath kept an evil diet long,
    And overmuch consumed his royal person:
    'Tis very grievous to be thought upon.
    What, is he in his bed?
HASTINGS. He is.
GLOUCESTER. Go you before, and I will follow you.—

[*Exit* HASTINGS.]

    He cannot live, I hope; and must not die
    Till George be pack'd with post-horse up to heaven.
    I'll in, to urge his hatred more to Clarence,
    With lies well steel'd with weighty arguments;
    And, if I fall not in my deep intent,
    Clarence hath not another day to live:
    Which done, God take King Edward to his mercy,
    And leave the world for me to bustle in!
    For then I'll marry Warwick's youngest daughter:[23]

---

[20] *Prevail'd* on is here used for *prevail'd against.*

[21] Fear *for* him, of course. This mode of speech was not uncommon.

[22] "By Saint Paul" was in fact Richard's favourite oath.

[23] This was Lady Anne, daughter of Richard Neville, the great Earl of Warwick, known in history as the "king-maker." She had been married to Edward, Prince of Wales, son of King Henry the Sixth. Her young husband was killed, murdered, it was said, at the battle of Tewksbury, which took place May 4th, 1471. Her oldest sister, Isabella, wife to the Clarence of this play, had died some time before.

What though I kill'd her husband and her father?
The readiest way to make the wench amends
Is to become her husband and her father:
The which will I; not all so much for love
As for another secret close intent,[24]
By marrying her which I must reach unto.
But yet I run before my horse to market:
Clarence still breathes; Edward still lives and reigns:
When they are gone, then must I count my gains. [*Exit.*]

SCENE II.

The Same. Another Street.

[*Enter the corpse of King* HENRY *the Sixth, borne in an open coffin, Gentlemen with halberds to guard it;—among them* TRESEEL *and* BERKELEY; *and Lady* ANNE *as Mourner.*]

LADY ANNE. Set down, set down your honourable load,—
If honour may be shrouded in a hearse,—
Whilst I awhile obsequiously[25] lament
The untimely fall of virtuous Lancaster.—

[*The Bearers set down the coffin.*]

Poor key-cold[26] figure of a holy king!
Pale ashes of the house of Lancaster!
Thou bloodless remnant of that royal blood!
Be it lawful that I invocate thy ghost,
To hear the lamentations of Poor Anne,
Wife to thy Edward, to thy slaughter'd son,
Stabb'd by the selfsame hand that made these wounds!
Lo, in these windows that let forth thy life,
I pour the helpless balm of my poor eyes.
Cursed be the hand that made these fatal holes!
Cursed be the heart that had the heart to do it!

---

[24] This "secret close intent" probably was to get into his hands the son and daughter of Clarence, who had been left in the care of Lady Anne their aunt, and had succeeded to the larger portion of the vast estates of their grandfather, the great Earl of Warwick.

[25] To lament *obsequiously* is to make the lamentation proper to *obsequies*, or rites of burial.

[26] As *cold* as a *key*; but why a key should be taken for an image of coldness is not very clear. The usage is not uncommon in the old writers. Shakespeare has it again in *Lucrece*: "And then in *key-cold* Lucrece' bleeding stream he falls." Thus, also, in Holland's Pliny: "In this habite, disguised as hee sat, hee was starke dead and *key-cold* before any man perceived it."

Cursed the blood that let this blood from hence!
More direful hap betide that hated wretch,
That makes us wretched by the death of thee,
Than I can wish to adders, spiders, toads,
Or any creeping venom'd thing that lives!
If ever he have child, abortive be it,
Prodigious,[27] and untimely brought to light,
Whose ugly and unnatural aspect
May fright the hopeful mother at the view;
And that be heir to his unhappiness![28]
If ever he have wife, let her he made
A miserable by the death of him
As I am made by my poor lord and thee!—
Come, now towards Chertsey with your holy load,
Taken from Paul's to be interred there;
And still, as you are weary of the weight,
Rest you, whiles I lament King Henry's corpse.

[*The Bearers take up the coffin and move forwards.*]

[*Enter* GLOUCESTER.]

GLOUCESTER. Stay, you that bear the corpse, and set it down.
LADY ANNE. What black magician conjures up this fiend,
To stop devoted charitable deeds?
GLOUCESTER. Villains, set down the corpse; or, by Saint Paul,
I'll make a corpse of him that disobeys.
GENTLEMAN. My lord, stand back, and let the coffin pass.
GLOUCESTER. Unmanner'd dog! stand thou, when I command:
Advance[29] thy halberd higher than my breast,
Or, by Saint Paul, I'll strike thee to my foot,
And spurn upon thee, beggar, for thy boldness.

[*The Bearers set down the coffin.*]

LADY ANNE. What, do you tremble? are you all afraid?
Alas, I blame you not; for you are mortal,
And mortal eyes cannot endure the Devil.—
Avaunt, thou dreadful minister of hell!

---

[27] *Prodigious* for *monstrous*; one of the Latin senses of the word. Such births were held to be of evil omen.

[28] *Unhappiness* here means *mischievousness*, or *propensity* to *mischief*. The Poet has it several times in this sense.

[29] Here, as often, *advance* is *raise* or *lift up.*—*Unmanner'd*, in the preceding line, is *unmannerly*, or *insolent.*

Thou hadst but power over his mortal body,
His soul thou canst not have; therefore be gone.
GLOUCESTER. Sweet saint, for charity, be not so curst.[30]
LADY ANNE. Foul devil, for God's sake, hence, and trouble us not;
For thou hast made the happy earth thy hell,
Fill'd it with cursing cries and deep exclaims.
If thou delight to view thy heinous deeds,
Behold this pattern of thy butcheries.—
O, gentlemen, see, see! dead Henry's wounds
Open their congeal'd mouths and bleed[31] afresh!—
Blush, Blush, thou lump of foul deformity;
For 'tis thy presence that exhales[32] this blood
From cold and empty veins, where no blood dwells;
Thy deed, inhuman and unnatural,
Provokes this deluge most unnatural.—
O God, which this blood madest, revenge his death!
O earth, which this blood drink'st revenge his death!
Either heaven with lightning strike the murderer dead,
Or earth, gape open wide and eat him quick,[33]
As thou dost swallow up this good king's blood
Which his hell-govern'd arm hath butchered!
GLOUCESTER. Lady, you know no rules of charity,
Which renders good for bad, blessings for curses.
LADY ANNE. Villain, thou know'st no law of God nor man:
No beast so fierce but knows some touch of pity.
GLOUCESTER. But I know none, and therefore am no beast.
LADY ANNE. O wonderful, when devils tell the truth!
GLOUCESTER. More wonderful, when angels are so angry.
Vouchsafe, divine perfection of a woman,
Of these supposed-evils, to give me leave,
By circumstance, but to acquit myself.
LADY ANNE. Vouchsafe, diffused[34] infection of a man,
For these known evils, but to give me leave,
By circumstance, to curse thy cursed self.
GLOUCESTER. Fairer than tongue can name thee, let me have

---

[30] *Curst* is *sharp-tongued*, or fierce and bitter of speech. Repeatedly so.

[31] This is founded on Holinshed's account of Henry's funeral: "The dead corps was conveied from the Tower to the church of saint Paule, and there laid on a beire or coffen bare-faced: the same in presence of the beholders *did bleed*. From thense he was caried to the Blackfriers, and *bled there* likewise."—It used to be thought that the body of a murdered person would bleed afresh, if touched or approached by the murderer.

[32] Shakespeare repeatedly has *exhale* in the sense of *draw out*. In *Henry V.* Pistol uses it imperatively, meaning, "draw thy sword."

[33] *Quick* is *alive* or *living*; so that the meaning is *swallow* him alive. So in *Hamlet*, v. 1: "Be buried *quick* with her, and so will I."

[34] *Diffused* sometimes meant *dark, obscure, uncouth*, or *confused*.

Some patient leisure to excuse myself.
LADY ANNE. Fouler than heart can think thee, thou canst make
No excuse current, but to hang thyself.
GLOUCESTER. By such despair, I should accuse myself.
LADY ANNE. And, by despairing, shouldst thou stand excused;
For doing worthy vengeance on thyself,
Which didst unworthy slaughter upon others.
GLOUCESTER. Say that I slew them not?
LADY ANNE. Why, then they are not dead:
But dead they are, and devilish slave, by thee.
GLOUCESTER. I did not kill your husband.
LADY ANNE. Why, then he is alive.
GLOUCESTER. Nay, he is dead; and slain by Edward's hand.
LADY ANNE. In thy foul throat thou liest: Queen Margaret saw
Thy murderous falchion smoking in his blood;
The which thou once didst bend against her breast,
But that thy brothers beat aside the point.
GLOUCESTER. I was provoked by her slanderous tongue,
Which laid their guilt[35] upon my guiltless shoulders.
LADY ANNE. Thou wast provoked by thy bloody mind.
Which never dreamt on aught but butcheries:
Didst thou not kill this King?
GLOUCESTER. I grant ye.
LADY ANNE. Dost grant me, hedgehog? then, God grant me too
Thou mayst be damned for that wicked deed!
O, he was gentle, mild, and virtuous!
GLOUCESTER. The fitter for the King of heaven, that hath him.
LADY ANNE. He is in heaven, where thou shalt never come.
GLOUCESTER. Let him thank me, that holp[36] to send him thither;
For he was fitter for that place than earth.
LADY ANNE. And thou unfit for any place but hell.
GLOUCESTER. Yes, one place else, if you will hear me name it.
LADY ANNE. Some dungeon.
GLOUCESTER. Your bed-chamber.
LADY ANNE. I'll rest betide the chamber where thou liest!
GLOUCESTER. So will it, madam till I lie with you.
LADY ANNE. I hope so.
GLOUCESTER. I know so. But, gentle Lady Anne,—
To leave this keen encounter of our wits,
And fall somewhat into a slower method,—
Is not the causer of the timeless[37] deaths

---

[35] The guilt of his brothers who slew the Prince.
[36] *Holp* or *holpen* is the old preterite form of the verb to *help*. It occurs very often in the English *Psalter*, which is a much older version of the Psalms than that in the Bible.

Of these Plantagenets, Henry and Edward,
    As blameful as the executioner?
LADY ANNE. Thou art the cause, and most accursed effect.[38]
GLOUCESTER. Your beauty was the cause of that effect;
    Your beauty: which did haunt me in my sleep
    To undertake the death of all the world,
    So I might live one hour in your sweet bosom.
LADY ANNE. If I thought that, I tell thee, homicide,
    These nails should rend that beauty from my cheeks.
GLOUCESTER. These eyes could never endure sweet beauty's wreck;
    You should not blemish it, if I stood by:
    As all the world is cheered by the sun,
    So I by that; it is my day, my life.
LADY ANNE. Black night o'ershade thy day, and death thy life!
GLOUCESTER. Curse not thyself, fair creature thou art both.
LADY ANNE. I would I were, to be revenged on thee.
GLOUCESTER. It is a quarrel most unnatural,
    To be revenged on him that loveth you.
LADY ANNE. It is a quarrel just and reasonable,
    To be revenged on him that slew my husband.
GLOUCESTER. He that bereft thee, lady, of thy husband,
    Did it to help thee to a better husband.
LADY ANNE. His better doth not breathe upon the earth.
GLOUCESTER. He lives that loves thee better than he could.
LADY ANNE. Name him.
GLOUCESTER. Plantagenet.
LADY ANNE. Why, that was he.
GLOUCESTER. The selfsame name, but one of better nature.
LADY ANNE. Where is he?
GLOUCESTER. Here. [*She spits at him.*] Why dost thou spit at me?
LADY ANNE. Would it were mortal poison, for thy sake!
GLOUCESTER. Never came poison from so sweet a place.
LADY ANNE. Never hung poison on a fouler toad.
    Out of my sight! thou dost infect my eyes.
GLOUCESTER. Thine eyes, sweet lady, have infected mine.
LADY ANNE. Would they were basilisks,[39] to strike thee dead!

---

[37] *Timeless*, here, is *untimely*. A frequent use of the word in Shakespeare's time. So in *Romeo and Juliet*, v. 3: "Poison, I see, hath been his *timeless* end." In the first speech of this scene, we have a like use of *helpless* for *unhelping* or *unavailing*: "I pour the *helpless* balm of my poor eyes."

[38] And most accursed *is the* effect; *effect* referring to *their death.*

[39] The Poet has several allusions to this imaginary power of the reptile, called basilisk from its having on the head some resemblance to a crown; the name being from the Greek, and signifying a little king. So Bacon, *Advancement of Learning*, xxi. 9: "For, as the fable goeth of the basilisk, that if he see you first, you die for it; but if you see him first, he dieth; so is it with deceits and evil arts."

GLOUCESTER. I would they were, that I might die at once;
    For now they kill me with a living death.
    Those eyes of thine from mine have drawn salt tears,
    Shamed their aspect with store of childish drops:
    These eyes that never shed remorseful[40] tear,—
    No, when my father York and Edward wept,
    To hear[41] the piteous moan that Rutland made
    When black-faced Clifford shook his sword at him;
    Nor when thy warlike father, like a child,
    Told the sad story of my father's death,
    And twenty times made pause to sob and weep,
    That all the standers-by had wet their cheeks
    Like trees bedash'd with rain;—in that sad time
    My manly eyes did scorn an humble tear;
    And what these sorrows could not thence exhale,
    Thy beauty hath, and made them blind with weeping.
    I never sued to friend nor enemy;
    My tongue could never learn sweet smoothing word;
    But now thy beauty is proposed my fee,
    My proud heart sues, and prompts my tongue to speak.

[*She looks scornfully at him.*]

    Teach not thy lips such scorn, for they were made
    For kissing, lady, not for such contempt.
    If thy revengeful heart cannot forgive,
    Lo, here I lend thee this sharp-pointed sword;
    Which if thou please to hide in this true bosom.
    And let the soul forth that adoreth thee,
    I lay it naked to the deadly stroke,
    And humbly beg the death upon my knee.

[*Gives her his sword, and lays his breast open, kneeling.*]

    Nay, do not pause; for I did kill King Henry,—

[*She offers at his breast with his sword.*]

    But 'twas thy beauty that provoked me.
    Nay, now dispatch; 'twas I that stabb'd young Edward,—

[*She again offers at his breast.*]

---

[40] *Remorse* was continually used for *pity*, *remorseful* for *pitiful*.

[41] Wept *at hearing*; the infinitive used gerundively. The Poet abounds in this usage.

But 'twas thy heavenly face that set me on.

[*She lets fall the sword.*]

Take up the sword again, or take up me.
LADY ANNE. Arise, dissembler: though I wish thy death,
   I will not be the executioner.
GLOUCESTER. Then bid me kill myself, and I will do it.

[*Rises, and takes up his sword.*]

LADY ANNE. I have already.
GLOUCESTER. Tush, that was in thy rage:
   Speak it again, and, even with the word,
   That hand, which, for thy love, did kill thy love,
   Shall, for thy love, kill a far truer love;
   To both their deaths thou shalt be accessary.
LADY ANNE. I would I knew thy heart.
GLOUCESTER. 'Tis figured in my tongue.
LADY ANNE. I fear me both are false.
GLOUCESTER. Then never man was true.
LADY ANNE. Well, well, put up your sword.
GLOUCESTER. Say, then, my peace is made.
LADY ANNE. That shall you know hereafter.
GLOUCESTER. But shall I live in hope?
LADY ANNE. All men, I hope, live so.
GLOUCESTER. Vouchsafe to wear this ring.
LADY ANNE. To take is not to give. [*She puts on the ring.*]
GLOUCESTER. Look, how this ring encompasseth finger.
   Even so thy breast encloseth my poor heart;
   Wear both of them, for both of them are thine.
   And if thy poor devoted suppliant may
   But beg one favour at thy gracious hand,
   Thou dost confirm his happiness for ever.
LADY ANNE. What is it?
GLOUCESTER. That it would please thee leave these sad designs
   To him that hath more cause to be a mourner,
   And presently repair to Crosby Place;
   Where—after I have solemnly interr'd
   At Chertsey monastery this noble king,
   And wet his grave with my repentant tears—

I will with all expedient[42] duty see you:
For divers unknown reasons. I beseech you,
Grant me this boon.
LADY ANNE. With all my heart; and much it joys me too,
To see you are become so penitent.—
Tressel and Berkeley, go along with me.
GLOUCESTER. Bid me farewell.
LADY ANNE. 'Tis more than you deserve;
But since you teach me how to flatter you,
Imagine I have said farewell already.

[*Exeunt Lady* ANNE, TRESSEL, *and* BERKELEY.]

GLOUCESTER. Sirs, take up the corpse.
GENTLEMEN. Towards Chertsey, noble lord?
GLOUCESTER. No, to White-Friars; there attend[43] my coming.

[*Exeunt all but* GLOUCESTER.]

Was ever woman in this humour woo'd?
Was ever woman in this humour won?
I'll have her;—but I will not keep her long.
What! I, that kill'd her husband and his father,
To take her in her heart's extremest hate,
With curses in her mouth, tears in her eyes,
The bleeding witness of her hatred by;
Having God, her conscience, and these bars against me,
And I nothing to back my suit at all,
But the plain devil and dissembling looks,
And yet to win her,—all the world to nothing![44]
Ha!
Hath she forgot already that brave prince,
Edward, her lord, whom I, some three months since,
Stabb'd in my angry mood at Tewksbury?[45]
A sweeter and a lovelier gentleman,
Framed in the prodigality of nature,

---

[42] *Expedient* for *expeditious*. Repeatedly so. So in *King John*, ii. 1: "His marches are *expedient* to this town."

[43] Here, as often, *attend* is *wait for* or *await*. So in *Coriolanus*, i. 1: "Your company to th' Capitol; where our greatest friends *attend* us!"

[44] "The chances against me were as all the world to nothing."

[45] This fixes the time of the scene to August, 1471. King Edward, however, is introduced in the second Act dying. That King died in April, 1483; consequently there is an interval between this Act and the next of almost twelve years. Clarence, who is represented in the preceding scene as committed to the Tower before the burial of King Henry VI., was in fact not confined till February, 1478, nearly seven years afterwards.

Young, valiant, wise, and, no doubt, right royal,
The spacious world cannot again afford
And will she yet abase[46] her eyes on me,
That cropp'd the golden prime of this sweet prince,
And made her widow to a woeful bed?
On me, whose all not equals Edward's moiety?
On me, that halt and am unshapen thus?
My dukedom to a beggarly denier,[47]
I do mistake my person all this while:
Upon my life, she finds, although I cannot,
Myself to be a marvellous proper[48] man.
I'll be at charges for a looking-glass,
And entertain some score or two of tailors,
To study fashions to adorn my body:
Since I am crept in favour with myself,
Will maintain it with some little cost.
But first I'll turn yon fellow in[49] his grave;
And then return lamenting to my love.—
Shine out, fair sun, till I have bought a glass,
That I may see my shadow as I pass. [*Exit.*]

SCENE III.

The Same. A Room in the Palace.

[*Enter Queen* ELIZABETH, RIVERS, *and* GREY.]

RIVERS. Have patience, madam: there's no doubt his majesty
　　Will soon recover his accustom'd health.
GREY. In that you brook it in, it makes him worse:
　　Therefore, for God's sake, entertain good comfort,
　　And cheer his grace with quick[50] and merry words.
QUEEN ELIZABETH. If he were dead, what would betide of me?
RIVERS. No other harm but loss of such a lord.
QUEEN ELIZABETH. The loss of such a lord includes all harm.
GREY. The heavens have bless'd you with a goodly son,
　　To be your comforter when he is gone.
QUEEN ELIZABETH. Oh, he is young and his minority
　　Is put unto the trust of Richard Gloucester,

---

[46] To *abase* is to *cast down*, to *lower*, or to *let fall*.
[47] A small coin, the twelfth part of a French *sous*.
[48] *Marvellous* is here used adverbially. *Proper* for *handsome* or *well-proportioned*.
[49] Shakespeare uses *in* or *into* indifferently, as suits his verse.
[50] *Quick*, here, is *lively*, *sprightly*. So in *Love's Labours Lost*, i. 1: "But is there no *quick* recreation granted?"

A man that loves not me, nor none of you.

RIVERS. Is it concluded that he shall be protector?

QUEEN ELIZABETH. It is determined, not concluded[51] yet:
But so it must be, if the king miscarry.

[*Enter* BUCKINGHAM *and* STANLEY.[52]]

GREY. Here come the lords of Buckingham and Derby.

BUCKINGHAM. Good time of day unto your royal grace!

STANLEY. God make your majesty joyful as you have been!

QUEEN ELIZABETH. The Countess Richmond,[53] good my Lord of
Derby.
To your good prayers will scarcely say amen.
Yet, Derby, notwithstanding she's your wife,
And loves not me, be you, good lord, assured
I hate not you for her proud arrogance.

STANLEY. I do beseech you, either not believe
The envious slanders of her false accusers;
Or, if she be accused in true report,
Bear with her weakness, which, I think proceeds
From wayward sickness, and no grounded malice.

RIVERS. Saw you the king to-day, my Lord of Derby?

STANLEY. But now the Duke of Buckingham and I
Are come from visiting his majesty.

QUEEN ELIZABETH. What likelihood of his amendment, lords?

BUCKINGHAM. Madam, good hope; his grace speaks cheerfully.

QUEEN ELIZABETH. God grant him health! Did you confer with
him?

BUCKINGHAM. Madam, we did: he desires to make atonement[54]
Betwixt the Duke of Gloucester and your brothers,
And betwixt them and my lord chamberlain;

---

[51] A thing was said to be *determined*, when it was *resolved* upon; *concluded*, when it was *formally passed*, so as to be a ground of action.

[52] Henry Stafford, the present Duke of Buckingham, was descended, on his father's side, from Thomas of Woodstock, the fifth son of Edward III. On his mother's side he was descended from John of Ghent, third son of the same great Edward. He was as accomplished and as unprincipled as he was nobly descended.—Thomas Lord Stanley was Lord Steward of the King's household to Edward IV.

[53] The Countess of Richmond was Margaret, the only child of John Beaufort, the first Duke of Somerset, and so was descended from John of Ghent through the Beaufort branch of his family. See *3 Henry VI*, iv. VI. Margaret's first husband was Edmund, Earl of Richmond, son of Owen Tudor, by whom she became the mother of Henry VII. Afterwards she was married successively to Sir Henry Stafford, uncle of Buckingham, and to the Lord Stanley of this play, but had no more children. She lived to a great age, and was so highly reputed for prudence and virtue, that her grandson, Henry VIII., was mainly guided by her advice in forming his first council.

[54] *Atonement* is *reconciliation, at-one-ment*.

And sent to warn[55] them to his royal presence.
QUEEN ELIZABETH. Would all were well! but that will never be
    I fear our happiness is at the highest.

[*Enter* GLOUCESTER, HASTINGS, *and* DORSET.]

GLOUCESTER. They do me wrong, and I will not endure it:
    Who are they that complain unto the king,
    That I, forsooth, am stern, and love them not?
    By holy Paul, they love his grace but lightly
    That fill his ears with such dissentious rumours.
    Because I cannot flatter and speak fair,
    Smile in men's faces, smooth, deceive and cog,[56]
    Duck with French nods and apish courtesy,
    I must be held a rancorous enemy.
    Cannot a plain man live and think no harm,
    But thus his simple truth must be abused
    By silken, sly, insinuating Jacks?
RIVERS. To whom in all this presence speaks your Grace?
GLOUCESTER. To thee, that hast nor honesty nor grace.
    When have I injured thee? when done thee wrong?
    Or thee?—or thee?—or any of your faction?
    A plague upon you all! His royal Grace—
    Whom God preserve better than you would wish!—
    Cannot be quiet scarce a breathing-while,
    But you must trouble him with lewd[57] complaints.
QUEEN ELIZABETH. Brother of Gloucester, you mistake the matter.
    The king, of his own royal disposition,
    And not provoked by any suitor else;
    Aiming, belike, at your interior hatred,
    Which in your outward actions shows itself
    Against my kindred, brothers, and myself,
    Makes him to send; that thereby he may gather
    The ground of your ill-will, and so remove it.
GLOUCESTER. I cannot tell: the world is grown so bad,
    That wrens make prey where eagles dare not perch:
    Since every Jack became a gentleman
    There's many a gentle person made a Jack.[58]

---

[55] To *warn* was used for to *summon*.
[56] To *smooth*, or to *soothe*, is, in old language, to *insinuate* and *beguile* with flattery; to *cog*, is to *cajole* and *cheat*. Repeatedly so.
[57] *Lewd* in its old sense of *knavish*, *wicked*, or *base*.
[58] *Jack* was a common term of contempt or reproach. Richard is referring to the Queen's kindred, her sons, the Greys, and her brothers, the Woodvilles, who, by her

QUEEN ELIZABETH. Come, come, we know your meaning, brother
    Gloucester;
    You envy my advancement and my friends':
    God grant we never may have need of you!
GLOUCESTER. Meantime, God grants that we have need of you:
    Your brother is imprison'd by your means,
    Myself disgraced, and the nobility
    Held in contempt; whilst many fair promotions
    Are daily given to ennoble those
    That scarce, some two days since, were worth a noble.
QUEEN ELIZABETH. By Him that raised me to this careful height
    From that contented hap which I enjoy'd,
    I never did incense his majesty
    Against the Duke of Clarence, but have been
    An earnest advocate to plead for him.
    My lord, you do me shameful injury,
    Falsely to draw me in these vile suspects.
GLOUCESTER. You may deny that you were not the cause
    Of my Lord Hastings' late imprisonment.
RIVERS. She may, my lord, for—
GLOUCESTER. She may, Lord Rivers! why, who knows not so?
    She may do more, sir, than denying that:
    She may help you to many fair preferments,
    And then deny her aiding hand therein,
    And lay those honours on your high deserts.
    What may she not? She may,—ay, marry, may she,—
RIVERS. What, marry, may she?
GLOUCESTER. What, marry, may she! marry with a king,
    A bachelor, a handsome stripling too:
    I wis[59] your grandam had a worser match.
QUEEN ELIZABETH. My Lord of Gloucester, I have too long borne
    Your blunt upbraidings and your bitter scoffs:
    By heaven, I will acquaint his majesty
    With those gross taunts I often have endured.
    I had rather be a country servant-maid
    Than a great queen, with this condition,
    To be thus taunted, scorn'd, and baited at:

    [*Enter Queen* MARGARET, *behind.*]

---

marriage with the King, were suddenly raised from a far inferior rank to all but the
highest.

    [59] Dyce thinks that the writers of Shakespeare's time used *I wis* "as equivalent to *I
ween.*" Here it seems to have about the sense of *I think, I guess,* or, as they say at the
South, *I reckon.*

Small joy have I in being England's queen.

QUEEN MARGARET. [*Aside.*] And lessen'd be that small, God, I
    beseech thee!

Thy honour, state and seat is due to me.

GLOUCESTER. What! threat you me with telling of the king?
    Tell him, and spare not: look, what I have said
    I will avouch in presence of the king:
    I dare adventure to be sent to the Tower.
    'Tis time to speak; my pains are quite forgot.

QUEEN MARGARET. [*Aside.*] Out, devil! I remember them too well:
    Thou slewest my husband Henry in the Tower,
    And Edward, my poor son, at Tewksbury.

GLOUCESTER. Ere you were queen, yea, or your husband king,
    I was a pack-horse in his great affairs;
    A weeder-out of his proud adversaries,
    A liberal rewarder of his friends:
    To royalize his blood I spilt mine own.

QUEEN MARGARET. [*Aside.*] Yea, and much better blood than his or
    thine.

GLOUCESTER. In all which time you and your husband Grey
    Were factious for the House of Lancaster;—
    And, Rivers, so were you:—was not your husband
    In Margaret's battle[60] at Saint Alban's slain?
    Let me put in your minds, if you forget,
    What you have been ere now, and what you are;
    Withal, what I have been, and what I am.

QUEEN MARGARET. [*Aside.*] A murderous villain, and so still thou
    art.

GLOUCESTER. Poor Clarence did forsake his father, Warwick;
    Yea, and forswore himself,—which Jesu pardon!—

QUEEN MARGARET. [*Aside.*] Which God revenge!

GLOUCESTER.—To fight on Edward's party for the crown;
    And for his meed, poor lord, he is mew'd up.
    I would to God my heart were flint, like Edward's;
    Or Edward's soft and pitiful, like mine

---

[60] *Battle* here probably means *army*. A common use of the word in old writers.—Sir
John Grey, the Queen's former husband, fell in what is known as the second battle of
Saint Alban's, which took place February 18, 1461. In that battle the Lancastrians were
victorious, Queen Margaret being at the head of the army on that side. Their advantage,
however, was much more than lost at the great battle of Towton, fought on the 29th of
March following, and one of the fiercest and bloodiest in the long series of wars known
as the Wars of the Roses. Upon this triumph of the Yorkists, many of the Lancastrians,
and among them the Greys, were attainted, and stripped of their possessions. It was upon
her throwing herself at the feet of King Edward, and soliciting a reversal of the attainder
in behalf of her destitute children, that the Lady Grey first won his pity, which soon
warmed into love.

I am too childish-foolish for this world.

QUEEN MARGARET. [*Aside.*] Hie thee to hell for shame, and leave
    the world,
    Thou cacodemon![61] there thy kingdom is.

RIVERS. My Lord of Gloucester, in those busy days
    Which here you urge to prove us enemies,
    We follow'd then our lord, our lawful king:
    So should we you, if you should be our king.

GLOUCESTER. If I should be! I had rather be a pedlar:
    Far be it from my heart, the thought of it!

QUEEN ELIZABETH. As little joy, my lord, as you suppose
    You should enjoy, were you this country's king,
    As little joy may you suppose in me.
    That I enjoy, being the queen thereof.

QUEEN MARGARET. [*Aside.*] A little joy enjoys the queen thereof;
    For I am she, and altogether joyless.
    I can no longer hold me patient. [*Advancing.*]
    Hear me, you wrangling pirates, that fall out
    In sharing that which you have pill'd[62] from me!
    Which of you trembles not that looks on me?
    If not, that, I being queen, you bow like subjects,
    Yet that, by you deposed, you quake like rebels?—
    [*To* RICHARD.] O gentle villain, do not turn away!

GLOUCESTER. Foul wrinkled witch, what makest[63] thou in my sight?

QUEEN MARGARET. But repetition of what thou hast marr'd;
    That will I make before I let thee go.

GLOUCESTER. Wert thou not banished on pain of death?[64]

QUEEN MARGARET. I was; but I do find more pain in banishment
    Than death can yield me here by my abode.
    A husband and a son thou owest to me,—
    And thou a kingdom,—all of you allegiance:
    The sorrow that I have, by right is yours,
    And all the pleasures you usurp are mine.

GLOUCESTER. The curse my noble father laid on thee,
    When thou didst crown his warlike brows with paper

---

[61] A *cacodemon* is an evil spirit, a fiend. The word is Greek.

[62] To *pill* is to *pillage*. It is often used with to *poll* or *strip*. "Kildare did use to *pill* and *poll* his friendes, tenants, and reteyners."—HOLINSHED.

[63] "What *makest* thou" is old language for "what *doest* thou." Here it means, "what business have you in this place?"—*Gentle*, in the line before, is *high-born*.

[64] Margaret fled into France after the battle of Hexham, in 1464, and Edward issued a proclamation prohibiting any of his subjects from aiding her return, or harbouring her, should she attempt to revisit England. She remained abroad till April, 1471, when she landed at Weymouth. After the battle of Tewksbury, in May, 1471, she was confined in the Tower, where she continued a prisoner till 1475, when she was ransomed by her father Reignier, and removed to France, where she died in 1482.

And with thy scorns drew'st rivers from his eyes,
And then, to dry them, gavest the duke a clout
Steep'd in the faultless blood of pretty Rutland;—
His curses, then from bitterness of soul
Denounced against thee, are all fall'n upon thee;
And God, not we, hath plagued thy bloody deed.[65]

QUEEN ELIZABETH. So just is God, to right the innocent.

HASTINGS. O, 'twas the foulest deed to slay that babe,
And the most merciless that e'er was heard of!

RIVERS. Tyrants themselves wept when it was reported.

DORSET. No man but prophesied revenge for it.

BUCKINGHAM. Northumberland, then present, wept to see it.

QUEEN MARGARET. What were you snarling all before I came,
Ready to catch each other by the throat,
And turn you all your hatred now on me?
Did York's dread curse prevail so much with heaven?
That Henry's death, my lovely Edward's death,
Their kingdom's loss, my woful banishment,
Could all but answer for that peevish brat?
Can curses pierce the clouds and enter Heaven?—
Why, then, give way, dull clouds, to my quick curses!—
If not by war, by surfeit die your king,
As ours by murder, to make him a king!
Edward thy son, which now is Prince of Wales,
For Edward my son, which was Prince of Wales,
Die in his youth by like untimely violence!
Thyself a queen, for me that was a queen,
Outlive thy glory, like my wretched self!
Long mayst thou live to wail thy children's loss;
And see another, as I see thee now,
Deck'd in thy rights, as thou art stall'd in mine!
Long die thy happy days before thy death;
And, after many lengthen'd hours of grief,
Die neither mother, wife, nor England's Queen!—
Rivers and Dorset, you were standers by,
And so wast thou, Lord Hastings,—when my son
Was stabb'd with bloody daggers: God, I pray him,
That none of you may live your natural age,
But by some unlook'd accident cut off!

GLOUCESTER. Have done thy charm, thou hateful wither'd hag!

QUEEN MARGARET. And leave out thee? stay, dog, for thou shalt
hear me.
If heaven have any grievous plague in store

---

[65] The matter here referred to is set forth at length in *III King Henry VI.*

Exceeding those that I can wish upon thee,
O, let them[66] keep it till thy sins be ripe,
And then hurl down their indignation
On thee, the troubler of the poor world's peace!
The worm of conscience still begnaw thy soul!
Thy friends suspect for traitors while thou livest,
And take deep traitors for thy dearest friends!
No sleep close up that deadly eye of thine,
Unless it be whilst some tormenting dream
Affrights thee with a hell of ugly devils!
Thou elvish-mark'd, abortive, rooting hog![67]
Thou that wast seal'd in thy nativity
The slave of nature and the son of hell!
Thou slander of thy mother's heavy womb!
Thou loathed issue of thy father's loins!
Thou rag of honour! thou detested—

GLOUCESTER. Margaret.

QUEEN MARGARET. Richard!

GLOUCESTER. Ha!

QUEEN MARGARET. I call thee not.

GLOUCESTER. I cry thee mercy then, for I had thought
That thou hadst call'd me all these bitter names.

QUEEN MARGARET. Why, so I did; but look'd for no reply.
O, let me make the period to my curse!

GLOUCESTER. 'Tis done by me, and ends in—Margaret.

QUEEN ELIZABETH. Thus have you breathed your curse against
yourself.

QUEEN MARGARET. Poor painted queen, vain flourish of my
fortune!
Why strew'st thou sugar on that bottled spider,[68]
Whose deadly web ensnareth thee about?
Fool, fool! thou whet'st a knife to kill thyself.
The time will come when thou shalt wish for me
To help thee curse that poisonous bunchback'd toad.

HASTINGS. False-boding woman, end thy frantic curse,
Lest to thy harm thou move our patience.

QUEEN MARGARET. Foul shame upon you! you have all moved

---

[66] *Them* refers to *Heaven*, the latter being a collective noun.

[67] She calls him *hog*, in allusion to his cognizance, which was a *boar*. "The expression," says Warburton, "is fine: remembering her youngest son, she alludes to the ravage which hogs make with the finest flowers in gardens; and intimating that Elizabeth was to expect no other treatment for her sons."—*Elvish-mark'd* refers to the old belief that deformities of person were the work of malignant or mischievous fairies or *elves*.

[68] Alluding to Richard's form and venom. A *bottled spider* is a *large, bloated spider*; supposed to contain venom in proportion to its size.

mine.

RIVERS. Were you well served, you would be taught your duty.

QUEEN MARGARET. To serve me well, you all should do me duty,
    Teach me to be your queen, and you my subjects:
    O, serve me well, and teach yourselves that duty!

DORSET. Dispute not with her; she is lunatic.

QUEEN MARGARET. Peace, master marquess, you are malapert:
    Your fire-new[69] stamp of honour is scarce current.
    O, that your young nobility could judge
    What 'twere to lose it, and be miserable!
    They that stand high have many blasts to shake them;
    And if they fall, they dash themselves to pieces.

GLOUCESTER. Good counsel, marry:—learn it, learn it, marquess.

DORSET. It toucheth you, my lord, as much as me.

GLOUCESTER. Yea, and much more: but I was born so high,
    Our eyrie[70] buildeth in the cedar's top,
    And dallies with the wind and scorns the sun.

QUEEN MARGARET. And turns the sun to shade;—alas! alas!—
    Witness my son, now in the shade of death;
    Whose bright out-shining beams thy cloudy wrath
    Hath in eternal darkness folded up.
    Your aery buildeth in our eyrie's nest.—
    O God, that seest it, do not suffer it!
    As it was won with blood, lost be it so!

BUCKINGHAM. Have done! for shame, if not for charity.

QUEEN MARGARET. Urge neither charity nor shame to me:
    Uncharitably with me have you dealt,
    And shamefully by you my hopes are butcher'd.
    My charity is outrage, life my shame;[71]
    And in that shame still live my sorrow's rage.

BUCKINGHAM. Have done, have done.

QUEEN MARGARET. O princely Buckingham I'll kiss thy hand,
    In sign of league and amity with thee:
    Now fair befal thee and thy noble house!
    Thy garments are not spotted with our blood,
    Nor thou within the compass of my curse.

BUCKINGHAM. Nor no one here; for curses never pass
    The lips of those that breathe them in the air.

---

[69] *Fire-new* is the old term for what we call *brand-new*.

[70] *Eyrie* for *brood*. This word properly signified a brood of eagles, or hawks; though in later times often used for the nest of those birds of prey. Its etymology is from *eyren*, eggs.

[71] "Outrage is the only charity shown me, and a life of shame, dishonour, is all the life permitted me." "*My* charity" may mean either the charity done *by* me or that done *to* me; here it means the latter.

QUEEN MARGARET. I'll not believe but they ascend the sky,
    And there awake God's gentle-sleeping peace.
    O Buckingham, take heed of yonder dog!
    Look, when he fawns, he bites; and when he bites,
    His venom tooth will rankle to the death:
    Have not to do with him, beware of him;
    Sin, death, and hell have set their marks on him,
    And all their ministers attend on him.
GLOUCESTER. What doth she say, my Lord of Buckingham?
BUCKINGHAM. Nothing that I respect, my gracious lord.
QUEEN MARGARET. What, dost thou scorn me for my gentle
    counsel?
    And soothe the devil that I warn thee from?
    O, but remember this another day,
    When he shall split thy very heart with sorrow,
    And say poor Margaret was a prophetess!—
    Live each of you the subjects to his hate,
    And he to yours, and all of you to God's! [*Exit.*]
HASTINGS. My hair doth stand on end to hear her curses.
RIVERS. And so doth mine: I muse[72] why she's at liberty.
GLOUCESTER. I cannot blame her: by God's holy mother,
    She hath had too much wrong; and I repent
    My part thereof that I have done to her.
QUEEN ELIZABETH. I never did her any, to my knowledge.
GLOUCESTER. But you have all the vantage of her wrong.
    I was too hot to do somebody good,
    That is too cold in thinking of it now.
    Marry, as for Clarence, he is well repaid,
    He is frank'd up[73] to fatting for his pains
    God pardon them that are the cause of it!
RIVERS. A virtuous and a Christian-like conclusion,
    To pray for them that have done scathe to us.
GLOUCESTER. So do I ever, being well-advised;[74]—
    [*Aside.*] For had I cursed now, I had cursed myself.

    [*Enter* CATESBY.]

CATESBY. Madam, his majesty doth call for you,—
    And for your Grace,—and you, my noble lords.

---

[72] To *muse* is, in old usage, to *marvel* or to *wonder*.

[73] A *frank* is a *pen* or *coop* in which hogs and other animals were confined while fatting. To be *franked up* was to be *closely confined*. To *franch*, or *frank*, was to stuff, to cram, or fatten.

[74] "Being well advised" is the same as having well considered, or, as we now say, speaking or acting advisedly.—*Scathe*, in the line before, is an old word for *harm*.

QUEEN ELIZABETH. Catesby, we come.—Lords, will you go with
    us?
RIVERS. Madam, we will attend your grace.

[*Exeunt all but* GLOUCESTER.]

GLOUCESTER. I do the wrong, and first begin to brawl.
    The secret mischiefs that I set abroach
    I lay unto the grievous charge of others.
    Clarence, whom I, indeed, have laid in darkness,
    I do beweep to many simple gulls
    Namely, to Hastings, Derby, Buckingham;
    And say it is the queen and her allies
    That stir the king against the duke my brother.
    Now, they believe it; and withal whet me
    To be revenged on Rivers, Vaughan, Grey:
    But then I sigh; and, with a piece of scripture,
    Tell them that God bids us do good for evil:
    And thus I clothe my naked villainy
    With old odd ends stolen out of holy writ;
    And seem a saint, when most I play the devil.
    But, soft! here come my executioners.—

[*Enter two* MURDERERS.]

    How now, my hardy, stout-resolvèd[75] mates!
    Are you now going to dispatch this deed?
FIRST MURDERER. We are, my lord; and come to have the warrant
    That we may be admitted where he is.
GLOUCESTER. Well thought upon; I have it here about me.

[*Gives the warrant.*]

    When you have done, repair to Crosby Place.
    But, sirs, be sudden in the execution,
    Withal obdurate, do not hear him plead;
    For Clarence is well-spoken, and perhaps
    May move your hearts to pity if you mark him.
FIRST MURDERER. Tush!
    Fear not, my lord, we will not stand to prate;
    Talkers are no good doers: be assured
    We come to use our hands and not our tongues.

---

[75] *Stout-resolvèd* is the same in sense as *boldly resolute*; or, as we might say, men of
iron resolution.

GLOUCESTER. Your eyes drop millstones,[76] when fools' eyes drop
 tears:
 I like you, lads; about your business straight;
 Go, go, dispatch.
FIRST MURDERER. We will, my noble lord. [*Exeunt.*]

SCENE IV.

The Same. A Room in the Tower.

[*Enter* CLARENCE *and* BRAKENBURY.]

BRAKENBURY. Why looks your grace so heavily today?
CLARENCE. O, I have pass'd a miserable night,
 So full of ugly sights, of ghastly dreams,
 That, as I am a Christian faithful man,
 I would not spend another such a night,
 Though 'twere to buy a world of happy days,
 So full of dismal terror was the time!
BRAKENBURY. What was your dream? I long to hear you tell it.
CLARENCE. Methoughts that I had broken from the Tower,
 And was embark'd to cross to Burgundy;[77]
 And, in my company, my brother Gloucester;
 Who from my cabin tempted me to walk
 Upon the hatches: thence we looked toward England,
 And cited up a thousand fearful times,
 During the wars of York and Lancaster
 That had befall'n us. As we paced along
 Upon the giddy footing of the hatches,
 Methought that Gloucester stumbled; and, in falling,
 Struck me, that thought to stay him, overboard,
 Into the tumbling billows of the main.
 O Lord! methought, what pain it was to drown!
 What dreadful noise of waters in mine ears!
 What ugly sights of death within mine eyes!
 Methought I saw a thousand fearful wrecks;
 Ten thousand men that fishes gnaw'd upon;
 Wedges of gold, great anchors, heaps of pearl,
 Inestimable stones, unvalued[78] jewels,

---

[76] *Weeping mill-stones* was a proverbial phrase used of persons not apt to weep. It occurs in the tragedy of *Cæsar and Pompey*, 1607. "Men's eyes must mill-stones drop, when fools shed tears."
 [77] Clarence was desirous to aid his sister Margaret against the French King, who invaded her jointure lands after the death of her husband, Charles Duke of Burgundy, who was killed at Nanci, in January, 1477.

All scatter'd in the bottom of the sea:
Some lay in dead men's skulls; and, in those holes
Where eyes did once inhabit, there were crept—
As 'twere in scorn of eyes—reflecting gems,
Which woo'd the slimy bottom of the deep,
And mock'd the dead bones that lay scatter'd by.
BRAKENBURY. Had you such leisure in the time of death,
To gaze upon the secrets of the deep?
CLARENCE. Methought I had; and often did I strive
To yield the ghost: but still the envious[79] flood
Kept in my soul, and would not let it forth
To seek the empty, vast and wandering air;
But smother'd it within my panting bulk,[80]
Which almost burst to belch it in the sea.
BRAKENBURY. Awaked you not with this sore agony?
CLARENCE. O, no, my dream was lengthen'd after life;
O, then began the tempest to my soul,
Who pass'd, methought, the melancholy flood,
With that grim ferryman which poets write of,
Unto the kingdom of perpetual night.
The first that there did greet my stranger soul,
Was my great father-in-law, renowned Warwick;
Who cried aloud, *What scourge for perjury*
Can this dark monarchy afford false Clarence?
And so he vanish'd: then came wandering by
A shadow like an angel, with bright hair
Dabbled in blood; and he squeak'd out aloud,
Clarence is come; false, fleeting,[81] *perjured Clarence,*
That stabb'd me in the field by Tewksbury;
Seize on him, Furies, take him to your torments!

---

[78] *Unvalued* for *invaluable*, not to be valued, inestimable.

[79] *Envious* in the sense of *malicious*, which was then its more common meaning. So in the preceding scene: "The *envious* slanders of her false accusers."

[80] *Bulk* was used for *breast*. So in *Hamlet*, ii. 2: "He raised a sigh so piteous and profound, that it did seem to shatter all his *bulk*, and end his being."—*Vast*, in the line before, is *void* or *waste*; like the Latin *vastus*.—The "wandering air" is the aerial expanse where the soul would be free to use its wings, and roam at large. So in the description of Raphael's voyage to the Earth, *Paradise Lost*, v. 267:

> He speeds, and through the vast ethereal sky
> Sails between worlds and worlds, with steady wing,
> Now on the polar winds, then with quick fan
> Winnows the buxom air.

[81] *Fleeting* or *flitting*, in old language, was used for *uncertain, inconstant, fluctuating*. Clarence broke his oath with the Earl of Warwick, and joined the army of his brother Edward.

With that, methoughts, a legion of foul fiends
Environ'd me about, and howled in mine ears
Such hideous cries, that with the very noise
I trembling waked, and for a season after
Could not believe but that I was in hell,
Such terrible impression made the dream.
BRAKENBURY. No marvel, my lord, though it affrighted you;
I promise, I am afraid to hear you tell it.
CLARENCE. O Brakenbury, I have done those things,
Which now bear evidence against my soul,
For Edward's sake; and see how he requites me!—
O God! if my deep prayers cannot appease thee,
But thou wilt be avenged on my misdeeds,
Yet execute thy wrath in me alone,
O, spare my guiltless wife[82] and my poor children!—
I pray thee, gentle keeper, stay by me;
My soul is heavy, and I fain would sleep.
BRAKENBURY. I will, my lord: God give your Grace good rest!—

[CLARENCE *sleeps in a chair.*]

Sorrow breaks seasons and reposing hours,
Makes the night morning, and the noon-tide night.
Princes have but their tides for their glories,
An outward honour for an inward toil;
And, for unfelt imagination,
They often feel a world of restless cares:[83]
So that, betwixt their tides and low names,
There's nothing differs but the outward fame.

[*Enter the two* MURDERERS.]

FIRST MURDERER. Ho! who's here?
BRAKENBURY. In God's name what are you, and how came you
hither?
FIRST MURDERER. I would speak with Clarence, and I came hither on
my legs.
BRAKENBURY. Yea, are you so brief?
SECOND MURDERER. O sir, it is better to be brief than
tedious. Show him our commission; talk no more.

---

[82] The wife of Clarence died before he was apprehended and confined in the Tower.
See page 22, note 23.
[83] For imaginary pleasures which are unfelt by them, they often endure a great
burden of restless cares, which they feel, to their cost.

[FIRST MURDERER *gives a paper to* BRAKENBURY, *who reads it.*]

BRAKENBURY. I am, in this, commanded to deliver
    The noble Duke of Clarence to your hands:
    I will not reason what is meant hereby,
    Because I will be guiltless of the meaning.
    Here are the keys, there sits the duke asleep:
    I'll to the king; and signify to him
    That thus I have resign'd my charge to you.
FIRST MURDERER. Do so, it is a point of wisdom: fare you well.

[*Exit* BRAKENBURY.]

SECOND MURDERER. What, shall we stab him as he sleeps?
FIRST MURDERER. No; then he will say 'twas done cowardly, when he wakes.
SECOND MURDERER. When he wakes! why, fool, he shall never wake till he judgment-day.
FIRST MURDERER. Why, then he will say we stabbed him sleeping.
SECOND MURDERER. The urging of that word *judgment* hath bred a kind of remorse in me.
FIRST MURDERER. What, art thou afraid?
SECOND MURDERER. Not to kill him, having a warrant for it; but to be damned for killing him, from which no warrant can defend us.
FIRST MURDERER. I thought thou hadst been resolute.
SECOND MURDERER. So I am, to let him live.
FIRST MURDERER. Back to the Duke of Gloucester, tell him so.
SECOND MURDERER. I pray thee, stay a while: I hope my holy humour will change; 'twas wont to hold me but while one would tell twenty.
FIRST MURDERER. How dost thou feel thyself now?
SECOND MURDERER. 'Faith, some certain dregs of conscience are yet within me.
FIRST MURDERER. Remember our reward, when the deed is done.
SECOND MURDERER. 'Zounds, he dies: I had forgot the reward.
FIRST MURDERER. Where is thy conscience now?
SECOND MURDERER. In the Duke of Gloucester's purse.
FIRST MURDERER. So when he opens his purse to give us our reward, thy conscience flies out.
SECOND MURDERER. Let it go; there's few or none will entertain it.
FIRST MURDERER. How if it come to thee again?
SECOND MURDERER. I'll not meddle with it: it is a dangerous thing: it makes a man a coward: a man cannot steal, but it accuseth him; he cannot swear, but it cheques him; he cannot lie with his

neighbour's wife, but it detects him: 'tis a blushing shamefaced spirit that mutinies in a man's bosom; it fills one full of obstacles: it made me once restore a purse of gold that I found; it beggars any man that keeps it: it is turned out of all towns and cities for a dangerous thing; and every man that means to live well endeavours to trust to himself and to live without it.

FIRST MURDERER. 'Zounds, it is even now at my elbow, persuading me not to kill the duke.

SECOND MURDERER. Take the devil in thy mind, and believe him not:[84] he would insinuate with thee but to make thee sigh.

FIRST MURDERER. Tut, I am strong-framed, he cannot prevail with me, I warrant thee.

SECOND MURDERER. Spoke like a tall fellow[85] that respects his reputation. Come, shall we to this gear?

FIRST MURDERER. Take him over the costard with the hilts[86] of thy sword, and then we will chop him in the malmsey-butt in the next room.

SECOND MURDERER. O excellent devise! make a sop[87] of him.

FIRST MURDERER. Hark! he stirs: shall I strike?

SECOND MURDERER. No, we'll reason[88] with him.

CLARENCE. [*Waking.*] Where art thou, keeper? give me a cup of wine.

SECOND MURDERER. You shall have wine enough, my lord, anon.

CLARENCE. In God's name, what art thou?

SECOND MURDERER. A man, as you are.

CLARENCE. But not, as I am, royal.

SECOND MURDERER. Nor you, as we are, loyal.

CLARENCE. Thy voice is thunder, but thy looks are humble.

SECOND MURDERER. My voice is now the king's, my looks mine own.

CLARENCE. How darkly and how deadly dost thou speak!

---

[84] *Him* refers to *conscience*, not to *Devil.*—To *insinuate with* is to *make friends with*, to *play upon*, to *beguile*. The idea of conscience trying to wheedle and steal a man out of the Devil's leading is a most Shakesperian stroke of art. And the grim humour of these hired cut-throats in thus jesting away the approaches of preventive remorse is a capital instance of the Poet's inwardness with Nature. For even so men often laugh and sport themselves through the perpetration of crime; the supremacy of the moral law, the self-assertive rights of conscience instinctively prompting them to such tricks of evasion. I can hardly think of any one particular wherein Shakespeare's moral sanity of genius is more pregnantly manifested.

[85] That is, a *bold, stout-hearted* fellow.

[86] *Hilts*, the plural form, was commonly used where we should use *hilt.*—*Costard*, of course, is put for *head*. The word properly means *apple*, and was thus applied from similarity of shape.

[87] A *sop* is anything soaked or steeped in liquor.

[88] Here, as often, to *reason* is to *talk* or *converse.*—*Soft!* second line before, is the old exclamative for *hold*! *stay*! or *not too fast*!

Your eyes do menace me: why look you pale?
Who sent you hither? Wherefore do you come?
BOTH. To, to, to—
CLARENCE. To murder me?
BOTH. Ay, ay.
CLARENCE. You scarcely have the hearts to tell me so,
    And therefore cannot have the hearts to do it.
    Wherein, my friends, have I offended you?
FIRST MURDERER. Offended us you have not, but the king.
CLARENCE. I shall be reconciled to him again.
SECOND MURDERER. Never, my lord; therefore prepare to die.
CLARENCE. Are you call'd forth from out a world of men
    To slay the innocent? What is my offence?
    Where are the evidence that do accuse me?
    What lawful quest[89] have given their verdict up
    Unto the frowning judge? or who pronounced
    The bitter sentence of poor Clarence' death?
    Before I be convict[90] by course of law,
    To threaten me with death is most unlawful.
    I charge you, as you hope to have redemption
    By Christ's dear blood shed for our grievous sins,
    That you depart and lay no hands on me
    The deed you undertake is damnable.
FIRST MURDERER. What we will do, we do upon command.
SECOND MURDERER. And he that hath commanded is the king.
CLARENCE. Erroneous vassal! the great King of kings
    Hath in the tables of his law commanded
    That thou shalt do no murder: and wilt thou, then,
    Spurn at his edict and fulfil a man's?
    Take heed; for he holds vengeance in his hands,
    To hurl upon their heads that break his law.
SECOND MURDERER. And that same vengeance doth he hurl on
    thee,
    For false forswearing and for murder too:
    Thou didst receive the holy sacrament,
    To fight in quarrel of the house of Lancaster.
FIRST MURDERER. And, like a traitor to the name of God,
    Didst break that vow; and with thy treacherous blade
    Unrip'dst the bowels of thy sovereign's son.
SECOND MURDERER. Whom thou wert sworn to cherish and
    defend.
FIRST MURDERER. How canst thou urge God's dreadful law to us,

---

[89] *Quest* here means a *jury of inquest.*
[90] *Convict* for *convicted.* Such shortened preterites are very frequent.

When thou hast broke it in so dear degree?

CLARENCE. Alas! for whose sake did I that ill deed?
For Edward, for my brother, for his sake: Why, sirs,
He sends ye not to murder me for this
For in this sin he is as deep as I.
If God will be revenged for this deed.
O, know you yet, he doth it publicly,
Take not the quarrel from his powerful arm;
He needs no indirect nor lawless course
To cut off those that have offended him.

FIRST MURDERER. Who made thee, then, a bloody minister,
When gallant-springing brave Plantagenet,
That princely novice, was struck dead by thee?

CLARENCE. My brother's love, the devil, and my rage.

FIRST MURDERER. Thy brother's love, our duty, and thy fault,
Provoke us hither now to slaughter thee.

CLARENCE. Oh, if you love my brother, hate not me;
I am his brother, and I love him well.
If you be hired for meed, go back again,
And I will send you to my brother Gloucester,
Who shall reward you better for my life
Than Edward will for tidings of my death.

SECOND MURDERER. You are deceived, your brother Gloucester
hates you.

CLARENCE. O, no, he loves me, and he holds me dear:
Go you to him from me.

BOTH. Ay, so we will.

CLARENCE. Tell him, when that our princely father York
Bless'd his three sons with his victorious arm,
And charged us from his soul to love each other,
He little thought of this divided friendship:
Bid Gloucester think of this, and he will weep.

FIRST MURDERER. Ay, millstones; as be lesson'd us to weep.

CLARENCE. O, do not slander him, for he is kind.

FIRST MURDERER. Right,
As snow in harvest. Thou deceivest thyself:
'Tis he that sent us hither now to slaughter thee.

CLARENCE. It cannot be; for when I parted with him,
He hugg'd me in his arms, and swore, with sobs,
That he would labour my delivery.

SECOND MURDERER. Why, so he doth, now he delivers thee
From this world's thraldom to the joys of heaven.

FIRST MURDERER. Make peace with God, for you must die, my
lord.

CLARENCE. Hast thou that holy feeling in thy soul,

To counsel me to make my peace with God,
And art thou yet to thy own soul so blind,
That thou wilt war with God by murdering me?
Ah, sirs, consider, he that set you on
To do this deed will hate you for the deed.
SECOND MURDERER. [*To First.*] What shall we do?
CLARENCE. Relent, and save your souls.
FIRST MURDERER. Relent! 'tis cowardly and womanish.
CLARENCE. Not to relent is beastly, savage, devilish.
Which of you, if you were a prince's son,
Being pent from liberty, as I am now,
If two such murderers as yourselves came to you,
Would not entreat for life?
My friend, I spy some pity in thy looks:
O, if thine eye be not a flatterer,
Come thou on my side, and entreat for me,
As you would beg, were you in my distress
A begging prince what beggar pities not?
SECOND MURDERER. Look behind you, my lord.
FIRST MURDERER. Ay, [*Stabbing him.*] thus, and thus: if all this will
not do,
I'll drown you in the malmsey-butt within.

[*Exit, with the body.*]

SECOND MURDERER. A bloody deed, and desperately dispatch'd!
How fain, like Pilate, would I wash my hands
Of this most grievous guilty murder done!

[*Re-enter* FIRST MURDERER.]

FIRST MURDERER. How now! what mean'st thou, that thou help'st
me not?
By heavens, the duke shall know how slack thou art!
SECOND MURDERER. I would he knew that I had saved his brother!
Take thou the fee, and tell him what I say;
For I repent me that the duke is slain. [*Exit.*]
FIRST MURDERER. So do not I: go, coward as thou art.
Now must I hide his body in some hole,
Until the duke take order for his burial:
And when I have my meed, I must away;
For this will out, and here I must not stay.[91] [*Exit.*]

---

[91] The Duke of Clarence was arraigned for treason before the Parliament, convicted,
and sentence of death passed upon him. This was in February, 1478, and a few days later

ACT II.

SCENE I.

London. A Room in the Palace.

[*Enter King* EDWARD IV, *led in sick, Queen* ELIZABETH, DORSET, RIVERS, HASTINGS, BUCKINGHAM, GREY, *and others.*]

KING EDWARD IV. Why, so: now have I done a good day's work:
 You peers, continue this united league:
 I every day expect an embassage
 From my Redeemer to redeem me hence;
 And now in peace my soul shall part[92] to heaven,
 Since I have set my friends at peace on earth.
 Rivers and Hastings, take each other's hand;
 Dissemble not your hatred, swear your love.[93]
RIVERS. By heaven, my heart is purged from grudging hate:
 And with my hand I seal my true heart's love.
HASTINGS. So thrive I, as I truly swear the like!
KING EDWARD IV. Take heed you dally not before your king;
 Lest he that is the supreme King of kings
 Confound your hidden falsehood, and award
 Either of you to be the other's end.
HASTINGS. So prosper I, as I swear perfect love!
RIVERS. And I, as I love Hastings with my heart!
KING EDWARD IV. Madam, yourself are not exempt in this,—
 Nor your son Dorset,—Buckingham, nor you;—
 You have been factious one against the other,
 Wife, love Lord Hastings, let him kiss your hand;
 And what you do, do it unfeignedly.
QUEEN ELIZABETH. Here, Hastings; I will never more remember
 Our former hatred, so thrive I and mine!
KING EDWARD IV. Dorset, embrace him;—Hastings, love lord
 marquess.

---

it was announced that he had died in the Tower. So that this first Act of the play embraces a period of nearly seven years, the death of King Henry having occurred in May, 1471. The manner of Clarence's death has never been ascertained. It was generally attributed to the machinations of Richard. There was a fierce grudge between the two Dukes, growing out of their rapacity towards the Warwick estates. See page 23, note 24.

[92] *Part* for *depart*; the two being often used indiscriminately.

[93] To *dissemble* is, strictly, to *put off* the show of what is, as to *simulate* is to *put on* the show of what is not. So here the meaning is, "Do not merely put off the show of hatred, but eradicate it altogether, and swear love into its place."

DORSET. This interchange of love, I here protest,
    Upon my part shall be inviolable.
HASTINGS. And so swear I. [*They embrace.*]
KING EDWARD IV. Now, princely Buckingham, seal thou this league
    With thy embracements to my wife's allies,
    And make me happy in your unity.
BUCKINGHAM. [*To the* QUEEN.] Whenever Buckingham doth turn his hate
    On you or yours, but[94] with all duteous love
    Doth cherish you and yours, God punish me
    With hate in those where I expect most love!
    When I have most need to employ a friend,
    And most assured that he is a friend
    Deep, hollow, treacherous, and full of guile,
    Be he unto me! this do I beg of God,
    When I am cold in zeal to yours.

    [*Embracing* RIVERS, *&c.*]

KING EDWARD IV. A pleasing cordial, princely Buckingham,
    Is this thy vow unto my sickly heart.
    There wanteth now our brother Gloucester here,
    To make the perfect period of this peace.
BUCKINGHAM. And, in good time, here comes the noble duke.

    [*Enter* GLOUCESTER.]

GLOUCESTER. Good morrow to my sovereign king and queen:
    And, princely peers, a happy time of day!
KING EDWARD IV. Happy, indeed, as we have spent the day.
    Brother, we done deeds of charity;
    Made peace enmity, fair love of hate,
    Between these swelling wrong-incensed peers.
GLOUCESTER. A blessed labour, my most sovereign liege:
    Amongst this princely heap,[95] if any here,
    By false intelligence, or wrong surmise, hold me
    A foe; if I unwittingly, or in my rage,
    Have aught committed that is hardly borne
    By any in this presence, I desire

---

[94] A very uncommon use of *but*, which is here equivalent to *and not*, or, better, to *or not*. The full sense appears to be, "Whenever Buckingham doth turn his hate upon you, *or rather* when he doth not with all duteous love," &c.

[95] *Heap* for *throng, crowd,* or *gathering,* occurs repeatedly. So in *Julius Cæsar,* i. 3: "And there were drawn upon a *heap* a hundred ghastly women, transformed with their fear."

To reconcile me to his friendly peace:
'Tis death to me to be at enmity;
I hate it, and desire all good men's love.—
First, madam, I entreat true peace of you,
Which I will purchase with my duteous service;—
Of you, my noble cousin Buckingham,
If ever any grudge were lodged between us;
Of you, Lord Rivers,—and, Lord Grey, of you;
That without desert have frown'd on me;—
Dukes, earls, lords, gentlemen;—indeed, of all.
I do not know that Englishman alive
With whom my soul is any jot at odds
More than the infant that is born to-night
I thank my God for my humility.
QUEEN ELIZABETH. A holy day shall this be kept hereafter:
I would to God all strifes were well compounded.
My sovereign liege, I do beseech your majesty
To take our brother Clarence to your grace.
GLOUCESTER. Why, madam, have I offer'd love for this
To be so flouted in this royal presence?
Who knows not that the noble duke is dead? [*They all start.*]
You do him injury to scorn his corpse.
RIVERS. Who knows not he is dead! who knows he is?
QUEEN ELIZABETH. All seeing heaven, what a world is this!
BUCKINGHAM. Look I so pale, Lord Dorset, as the rest?
DORSET. Ay, my good lord; and no one in this presence
But his red colour hath forsook his cheeks.
KING EDWARD IV. Is Clarence dead? the order was reversed.
GLOUCESTER. But he, poor soul, by your first order died,
And that a winged Mercury did bear:
Some tardy cripple bore the countermand,
That came too lag to see him buried.
God grant that some, less noble and less loyal,
Nearer in bloody thoughts, but not in blood,
Deserve not worse than wretched Clarence did,
And yet go current from suspicion!

[*Enter* STANLEY.]

DORSET. A boon, my sovereign, for my service done!
KING EDWARD IV. I pray thee, peace: my soul is full of sorrow.
DORSET. I will not rise, unless your highness grant.
KING EDWARD IV. Then speak at once what is it thou demand'st.

DORSET. The forfeit,[96] sovereign, of my servant's life;
   Who slew to-day a righteous gentleman
   Lately attendant on the Duke of Norfolk.
KING EDWARD IV. Have a tongue to doom my brother's death,
   And shall the same give pardon to a slave?
   My brother slew no man; his fault was thought,
   And yet his punishment was cruel death.
   Who sued to me for him? who, in my rage,
   Kneel'd at my feet, and bade me be advised?[97]
   Who spake of brotherhood? who spake of love?
   Who told me how the poor soul did forsake
   The mighty Warwick, and did fight for me?
   Who told me, in the field by Tewksbury
   When Oxford had me down, he rescued me,
   And said, *Dear brother, live, and be a king*?
   Who told me, when we both lay in the field
   Frozen almost to death, how he did lap me
   Even in his own garments, and gave himself,
   All thin and naked, to the numb cold night?
   All this from my remembrance brutish wrath
   Sinfully pluck'd, and not a man of you
   Had so much grace to put it in my mind.
   But when your carters or your waiting-vassals
   Have done a drunken slaughter, and defaced
   The precious image of our dear Redeemer,
   You straight are on your knees for pardon, pardon;
   And I unjustly too, must grant it you
   But for my brother not a man would speak,
   Nor I, ungracious, speak unto myself
   For him, poor soul. The proudest of you all
   Have been beholding[98] to him in his life;
   Yet none of you would once plead for his life.—
   O God, I fear thy justice will take hold
   On me, and you, and mine, and yours for this!—
   Come, Hastings, help me to my closet.—Ah,
   Poor Clarence!

[*Exeunt the* KING, *the* QUEEN, HASTINGS, RIVERS, DORSET,
   and GREY.]

---

[96] He means a remission of the *forfeit*; the servant having *forfeited* his life by the act of homicide.

[97] *Advised*, again, for *considerate*, or *cautious*. See page 40, note 74.

[98] *Beholding* where we should use *beholden*. Always so in Shakespeare. The word means *obliged* or *indebted*.

GLOUCESTER. This is the fruit of rashness! Mark'd you not
  How that the guilty kindred of the queen
  Look'd pale when they did hear of Clarence' death?
  O, they did urge it still unto the king!
  God will revenge it. But come, let us in,
  To comfort Edward with our company.
BUCKINGHAM. We wait upon your grace. [*Exeunt.*]

SCENE II.

The Same. Another Room in the Palace.

[*Enter the* DUCHESS *of* York,[99] *with a* SON *and* DAUGHTER *of*
CLARENCE.]

BOY. Tell me, good grandam, is our father dead?
DUCHESS OF YORK. No, boy.
BOY. Why do you wring your hands, and beat your breast,
  And cry *O Clarence, my unhappy son*!
GIRL. Why do you look on us, and shake your head,
  And call us wretches, orphans, castaways
  If that our noble father be alive?
DUCHESS OF YORK. My pretty cousins,[100] you mistake me much;
  I do lament the sickness of the king.
  As loath to lose him, not your father's death;
  It were lost sorrow to wail one that's lost.
BOY. Then, grandam, you conclude that he is dead.
  The king my uncle is to blame for this:
  God will revenge it; whom I will importune
  With daily prayers all to that effect.
GIRL. And so will I.
DUCHESS OF YORK. Peace, children, peace! the king doth love you
          well:
  Incapable[101] and shallow innocents,
  You cannot guess who caused your father's death.
BOY. Grandam, we can; for my good uncle Gloucester
  Told me, the king, provoked by the queen,

---

[99] Cicely, daughter of Ralph Neville, first Earl of Westmoreland, and widow of Richard Duke of York, who was killed at the battle of Wakefield, 1460. She survived her husband thirty-five years, living till the year 1495.

[100] The Duchess is speaking to her grandchildren, *cousin* being then used for this relation, as well as for *nephew*, *niece*, and indeed for *kindred* generally. The word *grandchild* does not occur in Shakespeare.

[101] *Incapable* is here used nearly, if not exactly, in the sense of *unconscious*; meaning that unconsciousness of evil which renders children *unsuspecting*. So in *Hamlet*, iv. 4: "As one *incapable* of her own distress."

Devised impeachments to imprison him:
And when my uncle told me so, he wept,
And hugg'd me in his arm, and kindly kiss'd my cheek;
Bade me rely on him as on my father,
And he would love me dearly as his child.

DUCHESS OF YORK. Oh, that deceit should steal such gentle[102] shapes,
And with a virtuous vizard hide foul guile!
He is my son; yea, and therein my shame;
Yet from my dugs[103] he drew not this deceit.

BOY. Think you my uncle did dissemble,[104] grandam?

DUCHESS OF YORK. Ay, boy.

BOY. I cannot think it. Hark! what noise is this?

[*Enter Queen* ELIZABETH, *distractedly*; RIVERS, *and* DORSET *following her.*]

QUEEN ELIZABETH. Oh, who shall hinder me to wail and weep,
To chide my fortune, and torment myself?
I'll join with black despair against my soul,
And to myself become an enemy.

DUCHESS OF YORK. What means this scene of rude impatience?[105]

QUEEN ELIZABETH. To make an act of tragic violence:
Edward, my lord, your son, our king, is dead.
Why grow the branches now the root is wither'd?
Why wither not the leaves the sap being gone?
If you will live, lament; if die, be brief,[106]
That our swift-winged souls may catch the king's;
Or, like obedient subjects, follow him
To his new kingdom of perpetual rest.

DUCHESS OF YORK. Ah, so much interest have I in thy sorrow
As I had title in thy noble husband!
I have bewept a worthy husband's death,

---

[102] *Gentle* here means *well-born* or *high-born*, as opposed to *simple* or *lowborn*. So in i. 3, of this play: "Ah, *gentle villain*, do not turn away." Spoken to Richard by Margaret.

[103] This word was formerly thought good enough for the most refined lips and the choicest strains of poetry.

[104] *Dissemble* was used, as it still is, both for *feigning* and for *concealing* thoughts and feelings. Here it has the sense of to *simulate* or to *feign*. See page 50, note 93.

[105] The endings -*ience* and -*iance*, as well as -*ion*, -*ian*, and -*ious*, are often used as two syllables by Shakespeare, especially at the end of a verse. So, here, impatience is, properly, four syllables. And so in the preceding scenes we have the line, "Lest to thy harm thou move our *patience*," and the line, "And, for unfelt imaginations"; where -*ience* and -*ions* are strictly dissyllabic.

[106] That is, "be *quick*." *Brief* is often used so, as also *briefly* for quickly. So in *Macbeth*, ii. 1: "Let's *briefly* put on manly readiness."

And lived by looking on his images:[107]
But now two mirrors of his princely semblance
Are crack'd in pieces by malignant death,
And I for comfort have but one false glass,
Which grieves me when I see my shame in him.
Thou art a widow; yet thou art a mother,
And hast the comfort of thy children left thee:
But death hath snatch'd my husband from mine arms,
And pluck'd two crutches from my feeble limbs,
Edward and Clarence. O, what cause have I—
Thine being but a moiety of my grief—
To overgo thy plaints and drown thy cries!

SON. Good aunt, you wept not for our father's death;
How can we aid you with our kindred tears?

DAUGHTER. Our fatherless distress was left unmoan'd;
Your widow-dolour likewise be unwept!

QUEEN ELIZABETH. Give me no help in lamentation;
I am not barren to bring forth complaints
All springs reduce[108] their currents to mine eyes,
That I, being govern'd by the watery moon,
May send forth plenteous tears to drown the world!
Oh for my husband, for my dear lord Edward!

CHILDREN. Oh for our father, for our dear lord Clarence!

DUCHESS OF YORK. Alas for both, both mine, Edward and
Clarence!

QUEEN ELIZABETH. What stay had I but Edward? and he's gone.

CHILDREN. What stay had we but Clarence? and he's gone.

DUCHESS OF YORK. What stays had I but they? and they are gone.

QUEEN ELIZABETH. Was never widow had so dear a loss!

CHILDREN. Were never orphans had so dear a loss!

DUCHESS OF YORK. Was never mother had so dear a loss!
Alas, I am the mother of these moans!
Their woes are parcell'd, mine are general.
She for an Edward weeps, and so do I;
I for a Clarence weep, so doth not she:
These babes for Clarence weep and so do I;
I for an Edward weep, so do not they:
Alas, you three, on me, threefold distress'd,
Pour all your tears! I am your sorrow's nurse,
And I will pamper it with lamentations.

DORSET. Comfort, dear mother: God is much displeased

---

[107] "His *images*" are the *children* who represented and resembled him.

[108] *Reduce* in the Latin sense of *lead* or *bring back*. Repeatedly so. In the next line, the Moon is called *watery* from her connection with the tides. In *Hamlet*, i. 1, she is called "the *moist* star," for the same reason.

That you take with unthankfulness, his doing:
In common worldly things, 'tis call'd ungrateful,
With dull unwilligness to repay a debt
Which with a bounteous hand was kindly lent;
Much more to be thus opposite with heaven,
For it requires the royal debt it lent you.
RIVERS. Madam, bethink you, like a careful mother,
Of the young prince your son: send straight for him
Let him be crown'd; in him your comfort lives:
Drown desperate sorrow in dead Edward's grave,
And plant your joys in living Edward's throne.

[*Enter* GLOUCESTER, BUCKINGHAM, STANLEY, HAST-
INGS, RATCLIFF, *and others.*]

GLOUCESTER. Madam, have comfort: all of us have cause
To wail the dimming of our shining star;
But none can cure their harms by wailing them.
Madam, my mother, I do cry you mercy;[109]
I did not see your grace: humbly on my knee
I crave your blessing.
DUCHESS OF YORK. God bless thee; and put meekness in thy mind,
Love, charity, obedience, and true duty!
GLOUCESTER. Amen;—[*Aside.*] and make me die a good old man!
That is the butt-end of a mother's blessing:
I marvel why her grace did leave it out.
BUCKINGHAM. You cloudy princes and heart-sorrowing peers,
That bear this mutual heavy load of moan,
Now cheer each other in each other's love
Though we have spent our harvest of this king,
We are to reap the harvest of his son.
The broken rancour of your high-swoln hearts,
But lately splinter'd, knit, and join'd together,
Must gently be preserved, cherish'd, and kept:[110]
Me seemeth good, that, with some little train,
Forthwith from Ludlow the young Prince be fet[111]
Hither to London, to be crown'd our king.

---

[109] "I cry you mercy" is an old phrase for "I ask your pardon."

[110] This passage is touched with a sort of grammatical paralysis, but the sense is not very obscure. Their hearts had been swollen high with rancour, but the rancour has been broken out of them; and as the broken parts have been but lately splintered, and knit and joined together, so the union must be gently preserved, &c.

[111] *Fet* is an old preterite form of *fetch*. The poet has it in several other instances.— Prince Edward, as Prince of Wales, was in fact living at this time under the governance of his maternal uncle, the Earl of Rivers, at Ludlow Castle; his presence being deemed necessary to restrain the Welshmen, who were something wild and apt to be disorderly.

RIVERS. Why with some little train, my Lord of Buckingham?
BUCKINGHAM. Marry, my lord, lest, by a multitude,
 The new-heal'd wound of malice should break out,
 Which would be so much the more dangerous
 By how much the Estate[112] is green and yet ungovern'd:
 Where every horse bears his commanding rein,
 And may direct his course as please himself,
 As well the fear of harm, as harm apparent,[113]
 In my opinion, ought to be prevented.
GLOUCESTER. I hope the king made peace with all of us
 And the compact is firm and true in me.
RIVERS. And so in me; and so, I think, in all:
 Yet, since it is but green, it should be put
 To no apparent likelihood of breach,
 Which haply by much company might be urged:
 Therefore I say with noble Buckingham,
 That it is meet so few should fetch the prince.
HASTINGS. And so say I.
GLOUCESTER. Then be it so; and go we to determine
 Who they shall be that straight shall post to Ludlow.—
 Madam,—and you, my mother,—will you go
 To give your censures[114] in this weighty business?
QUEEN ELIZABETH DUCHESS OF YORK. With all our harts.

  [*Exeunt all but* BUCKINGHAM *and* GLOUCESTER.]

BUCKINGHAM. My lord, whoever journeys to the Prince,
 For God's sake, let not us two be behind;
 For, by the way, I'll sort occasion,
 As index[115] to the story we late talk'd of,
 To part the queen's proud kindred from the king.
GLOUCESTER. My other self, my counsel's consistory,
 My oracle, my prophet! My dear cousin,
 I, like a child, will go by thy direction.
 Towards Ludlow then, for we'll not stay behind. [*Exeunt.*]

---

 [112] "The *Estate*" here means "the State." In reference to the governing part of the Commonwealth, the two words anciently had the same meaning.

 [113] *Apparent* in its old sense of *evident* or *manifest.* Repeatedly so.

 [114] That is, your *judgments*, your *opinions.*

 [115] The *index* of a book was formerly set at the beginning; hence, probably, the word came to be used in the sense of *opening* or *introduction.* So in iv. 4 of this play: "The flattering index of a direful pageant." And in *Othello*, ii. 1: "An *index* and obscure *prologue* to the history of lust and foul thoughts."—Sort, in the line before, is used for *select* or *pick.*

SCENE III.

The Same. A Street.

[*Enter two* CITIZENS, *meeting.*]

FIRST CITIZEN. Neighbour, well met: whither away so fast?
SECOND CITIZEN. I promise you, I scarcely know myself:
 Hear you the news abroad?
FIRST CITIZEN. Ay, that the king is dead.
SECOND CITIZEN. Bad news, by'r lady; seldom comes the better:
 I fear, I fear 'twill prove a troublous world.

[*Enter a third* CITIZEN.]

THIRD CITIZEN. Neighbours, God speed!
FIRST CITIZEN. Give you good morrow, sir.
THIRD CITIZEN. Doth this news hold of good King Edward's death?
SECOND CITIZEN. Ay, sir, it is too true; God help the while!
THIRD CITIZEN. Then, masters, look to see a troublous world.
FIRST CITIZEN. No, no; by God's good grace his son shall reign.
THIRD CITIZEN. Woe to the land that's govern'd by a child![116]
SECOND CITIZEN. In him there is a hope of government,
 That in his nonage council under him,
 And in his full and ripen'd years himself,
 No doubt, shall then and till then, govern well.[117]
FIRST CITIZEN. So stood the state when Henry the Sixth
 Was crown'd in Paris but at nine months old.
THIRD CITIZEN. Stood the state so? No, no, good friends, God wot;
 For then this land was famously enrich'd
 With politic grave counsel; then the king
 Had virtuous uncles to protect his grace.
FIRST CITIZEN. Why, so hath this, both by the father and mother.
THIRD CITIZEN. Better it were they all came by the father,
 Or by the father there were none at all;
 For emulation now, who shall be nearest,
 Will touch us all too near, if God prevent not.
 O, full of danger is the Duke of Gloucester!
 And the queen's sons and brothers haught and proud:
 And were they to be ruled, and not to rule,

---

[116] So in *Ecclesiastes*, x. 16: "Woe to thee, O land! when thy king is a child."
[117] We may hope well of his government in all circumstances; we may hope this of his Council while he is in his nonage, and of himself in his riper years.

This sickly land might solace as before.

FIRST CITIZEN. Come, come, we fear the worst; all shall be well.

THIRD CITIZEN. When clouds appear, wise men put on their cloaks;
 When great leaves fall, the winter is at hand;
 When the sun sets, who doth not look for night?
 Untimely storms make men expect a dearth.
 All may be well; but, if God sort[118] it so,
 'Tis more than we deserve, or I expect.

SECOND CITIZEN. Truly, the souls of men are full of dread:
 Ye cannot reason[119] almost with a man
 That looks not heavily and full of fear.

THIRD CITIZEN. Before the times of change, still[120] is it so:
 By a divine instinct men's minds mistrust
 Ensuing dangers; as by proof, we see
 The waters swell before a boisterous storm.
 But leave it all to God.—Whither away?

SECOND CITIZEN. Marry, we were sent for to the justices.

THIRD CITIZEN. And so was I: I'll bear you company. [*Exeunt.*]

SCENE IV.

The Same. A Room in the Palace.

[*Enter the* ARCHBISHOP *of York, the young* DUKE *of York,*
Queen ELIZABETH, *and the* DUCHESS *of York.*]

ARCHBISHOP OF YORK. Last night, I hear, they lay at
 Northampton;
 At Stony-Stratford will they be to-night:
 To-morrow, or next day, they will be here.

DUCHESS OF YORK. I long with all my heart to see the prince:
 I hope he is much grown since last I saw him.

QUEEN ELIZABETH. But I hear, no; they say my son of York
 Hath almost overta'en him in his growth.

YORK. Ay, mother; but I would not have it so.

DUCHESS OF YORK. Why, my young cousin, it is good to grow.

YORK. Grandam, one night, as we did sit at supper,
 My uncle Rivers talk'd how I did grow
 More than my brother: 'Ay,' quoth my uncle Gloucester,
 Small herbs have grace, great weeds do grow apace:
 And since, methinks, I would not grow so fast,

---

[118] If God *allot* or ordain it so. *Sort* in the Latin sense of *sors.*

[119] *Reason*, again, for *talk* or *converse.* See page 46, note 88.

[120] *Still*, here, is *always, continually.* Often so.

Because sweet flowers are slow and weeds make haste.

DUCHESS OF YORK. Good faith, good faith, the saying did not hold
   In him that did object the same to thee;
   He was the wretched'st thing when he was young,
   So long a-growing and so leisurely,
   That, if this rule were true, he should be gracious.

ARCHBISHOP OF YORK. Why, madam, so, no doubt, he is.

DUCHESS OF YORK. I hope he is; but yet let mothers doubt.

YORK. Now, by my troth, if I had been remember'd,
   I could have given my uncle's grace a flout,
   To touch his growth nearer than he touch'd mine.

DUCHESS OF YORK. How, my pretty York? I pray thee, let me hear
   it.

YORK. Marry, they say my uncle grew so fast
   That he could gnaw a crust at two hours old
   'Twas full two years ere I could get a tooth.
   Grandam, this would have been a biting jest.

DUCHESS OF YORK. I pray thee, pretty York, who told thee this?

YORK. Grandam, his nurse.

DUCHESS OF YORK. His nurse! why, she was dead ere thou wert
   born.

YORK. If 'twere not she, I cannot tell who told me.

QUEEN ELIZABETH. A parlous[121] boy:—go to, you are too shrewd.

ARCHBISHOP OF YORK. Good madam, be not angry with the child.

QUEEN ELIZABETH. Pitchers have ears.

ARCHBISHOP OF YORK. Here comes a messenger.—

[*Enter a* MESSENGER.]

   What news?

MESSENGER. Such news, my lord, as grieves me to unfold.

QUEEN ELIZABETH. How fares the prince?

MESSENGER. Well, madam, and in health.

DUCHESS OF YORK. What is thy news then?

MESSENGER. Lord Rivers and Lord Grey are sent to Pomfret,
   With them Sir Thomas Vaughan, prisoners.

DUCHESS OF YORK. Who hath committed them?

MESSENGER. The mighty dukes
   Gloucester and Buckingham.

QUEEN ELIZABETH. For what offence?

MESSENGER. The sum of all I can, I have disclosed;
   Why or for what these nobles were committed
   Is all unknown to me, my gracious lady.

---

[121] *Parlous* is a popular form of *perilous*; jocularly used for *alarming*.

QUEEN ELIZABETH. Ay me, I see the downfall of our house!
 The tiger now hath seized the gentle hind;
 Insulting tyranny begins to jet
 Upon the innocent and aweless[122] throne:
 Welcome, destruction, death, and massacre!
 I see, as in a map, the end of all.
DUCHESS OF YORK. Accursed and unquiet wrangling days,
 How many of you have mine eyes beheld!
 My husband lost his life to get the crown;
 And often up and down my sons were toss'd,
 For me to joy and weep their gain and loss:
 And being seated, and domestic broils
 Clean over-blown, themselves, the conquerors.
 Make war upon themselves; blood against blood,
 Self against self: O, preposterous
 And frantic outrage, end thy damned spleen;
 Or let me die, to look on death no more!
QUEEN ELIZABETH. Come, come, my boy; we will to sanctuary.—
 Madam, farewell.
DUCHESS OF YORK. I'll go along with you.
QUEEN ELIZABETH. You have no cause.
ARCHBISHOP OF YORK. [*To the* QUEEN.] My gracious lady, go;
 And thither bear your treasure and your goods.
 For my part, I'll resign unto your grace
 The seal I keep: and so betide to me
 As well I tender you and all of yours!
 Come, I'll conduct you to the sanctuary. [*Exeunt.*]

---

[122] *To jet upon* means here *boldly to encroach upon.* So in *Titus Andronicus*, ii. 1: "And think you not how dangerous it is to jet upon a prince's right?" And in an old manuscript play of *Sir Thomas More*: "It is hard when Englishmens pacience must be thus *jetted on* by straungers."—*Awless* is unreverenced, not looked upon with awe.

ACT III.

SCENE I.

London. A Street.

[*The trumpets sound. Enter the Prince of* WALES, GLOUCESTER, BUCKINGHAM, CARDINAL BOUR-CHIER,[123] CATESBY, *and others.*]

BUCKINGHAM. Welcome, sweet prince, to London, to your chamber.[124]
GLOUCESTER. Welcome, dear cousin, my thoughts' sovereign
    The weary way hath made you melancholy.
PRINCE. No, uncle; but our crosses on the way
    Have made it tedious, wearisome, and heavy
    I want more uncles here to welcome me.
GLOUCESTER. Sweet prince, the untainted virtue of your years
    Hath not yet dived into the world's deceit
    Nor more can you distinguish of a man
    Than of his outward show; which, God he knows,
    Seldom or never jumpeth[125] with the heart.
    Those uncles which you want were dangerous;
    Your grace attended to their sugar'd words,
    But look'd not on the poison of their hearts:
    God keep you from them, and from such false friends!
PRINCE. God keep me from false friends! but they were none.
GLOUCESTER. My lord, the mayor of London comes to greet you.

[*Enter the Lord* MAYOR *and his train.*]

LORD MAYOR. God bless your grace with health and happy days!
PRINCE. I thank you, good my lord;—and thank you all.—

[MAYOR *and his Train retire.*]

---

[123] Thomas Bourchier was made a Cardinal, and elected Archbishop of Canterbury in 1464. He died in 1486.

[124] London was anciently called *camera regis*, that is, *the king's chamber*. Thus in Buckingham's speech to the citizens as given by More: "The prince, by *this noble citie as his speciall chamber,* and the speciall well renowned citie of this realme, much honourable fame receiveth among all other nations."

[125] To *jump* with is to *agree* or *correspond* with. So in *I King Henry IV.*, i. 2: "Well, Hal, well; and in some sort it *jumps* with my humour."

> I thought my mother, and my brother York,
> Would long ere this have met us on the way
> Fie, what a slug is Hastings, that he comes not
> To tell us whether they will come or no!

[*Enter* HASTINGS.]

BUCKINGHAM. And, in good time, here comes the sweating lord.
PRINCE. Welcome, my lord: what, will our mother come?
HASTINGS. On what occasion, God he knows, not I,
> The queen your mother, and your brother York,
> Have taken sanctuary: the tender prince
> Would fain have come with me to meet your grace,
> But by his mother was perforce withheld.
BUCKINGHAM. Fie, what an indirect and peevish course
> Is this of hers!—Lord cardinal, will your grace
> Persuade the queen to send the Duke of York
> Unto his princely brother presently?
> If she deny,—Lord Hastings, go with him,
> And from her jealous arms pluck him perforce.
CARDINAL. My Lord of Buckingham, if my weak oratory
> Can from his mother win the Duke of York,
> Anon expect him here; but if she be obdurate
> To mild entreaties, God in heaven forbid
> We should infringe the holy privilege
> Of blessed sanctuary! not for all this land
> Would I be guilty of so deep a sin.
BUCKINGHAM. You are too senseless—obstinate, my lord,
> Too ceremonious and traditional;[126]
> Weigh it but with the grossness of this age.[127]
> You break not sanctuary in seizing him.
> The benefit thereof is always granted
> To those whose dealings have deserved the place,
> And those who have the wit to claim the place:
> This prince hath neither claim'd it nor deserved it;
> And therefore, in mine opinion, cannot have it:
> Then, taking him from thence that is not there,

---

[126] *Ceremonious* for *superstitious,* or *tenacious of formalities; traditional* for *adherent to received* customs.

[127] *Weigh* is in the same construction with *are* in the second line before, the copulative *and* being understood. And to *weigh,* as the word is here used, is to *judge* or to *consider.* So that the sense of the whole is, "You are too much swayed by popular forms and traditions, and you judge the matter only in accordance with the gross and undistinguishing superstition which now prevails." Such is, in substance, Heath's explanation of the passage.

You break no privilege nor charter there.
Oft have I heard of sanctuary men;
But sanctuary children ne'er till now.
CARDINAL. My lord, you shall o'er-rule my mind for once.—
Come on, Lord Hastings, will you go with me?
HASTINGS. I go, my lord.
PRINCE. Good lords, make all the speedy haste you may.—

[*Exeunt* CARDINAL *and* HASTINGS.]

Say, uncle Gloucester, if our brother come,
Where shall we sojourn till our coronation?
GLOUCESTER. Where it seems best unto your royal self.
If I may counsel you, some day or two
Your highness shall repose you at the Tower:
Then where you please, and shall be thought most fit
For your best health and recreation.
PRINCE. I do not like the Tower, of any place.—
Did Julius Caesar build that place, my lord?
BUCKINGHAM. He did, my gracious lord, begin that place;
Which, since, succeeding ages have re-edified.
PRINCE. Is it upon record, or else reported
Successively from age to age, he built it?
BUCKINGHAM. Upon record, my gracious lord.
PRINCE. But say, my lord, it were not register'd,
Methinks the truth should live from age to age,
As 'twere retail'd[128] to all posterity,
Even to the general all-ending day.
GLOUCESTER. [*Aside.*] So wise so young, they say, do never live long.
PRINCE. What say you, uncle?
GLOUCESTER. I say, without characters,[129] fame lives long.—
[*Aside.*] Thus, like the formal Vice,[130] Iniquity,

---

[128] That is, *recounted.* Minsheu, in his *Dictionary,* 1617, besides the verb *retail,* in the mercantile sense, has the verb to *retaile* or *retell.* Richard uses the word again in the fourth Act, when speaking to the Queen of her daughter: "To whom I will *retail* my conquests won."

[129] Without the help of *letters* or *inscriptions.*

[130] Of that distinguished personage, the Vice or jester of the old Moralities. His part appears to have been on all occasions much the same, consisting in a given round or *set form* of action; for which cause, probably, the epithet *formal* is here applied to him. The following is Gifford's description of him: "He appears to have been a perfect counterpart of the harlequin of the modern stage, and had a twofold office,—to instigate the hero of the piece to wickedness, and at the same time to protect him from the Devil, whom he was permitted to buffet and battle with his wooden sword, till the process of the story required that both the protector and the protected should be carried off by the fiend; or the

I moralize two meanings in one word.[131]

PRINCE. That Julius Caesar was a famous man;
  With what his valour did enrich his wit,
  His wit set down to make his valour live
  Death makes no conquest of this conqueror;
  For now he lives in fame, though not in life.—
  I'll tell you what, my cousin Buckingham,—
BUCKINGHAM. What, my gracious lord?
PRINCE. An if I live until I be a man,
  I'll win our ancient right in France again,
  Or die a soldier, as I lived a king.
GLOUCESTER. [*Aside.*] Short summers lightly[132] have a forward
  spring.

[*Enter* YORK, *with the* CARDINAL *and* HASTINGS.]

BUCKINGHAM. Now, in good time, here comes the Duke of York.
PRINCE. Richard of York! how fares our loving brother?
YORK. Well, my dread lord; so must I call you now.
PRINCE. Ay, brother,—to our grief, as it is yours:
  Too late[133] he died that might have kept that title,
  Which by his death hath lost much majesty.
GLOUCESTER. How fares our cousin, noble Lord of York?
YORK. I thank you, gentle uncle. O, my lord,
  You said that idle weeds are fast in growth
  The prince my brother hath outgrown me far.
GLOUCESTER. He hath, my lord.
YORK. And therefore is he idle?
GLOUCESTER. O, my fair cousin, I must not say so.
YORK. Then is he more beholding to you than I.
GLOUCESTER. He may command me as my sovereign;
  But you have power in me as in a kinsman.

---

latter driven roaring from the stage, by some miraculous interposition in favour of the repentant offender."

[131] Heath explains as follows: "Thus my moralities, or the sententious expressions I have just uttered, resemble those of the Vice, Iniquity, in the play; the indecencies which lie at the bottom are sheltered from exception and the indignation they would excite if nakedly delivered, under the ambiguity of a double meaning." The writer adds, "The term moralize is only introduced in allusion to the title of our old dramatic pieces, which were commonly called *Moralities*, in which the Vice was always one of the shining characters." It is to be noted further, that, as the Vice acted the part of a buffoon or jester, he was wont "to deal largely in double meanings, and by the help of them to aim at cracking a jest or raising a laugh."

[132] *Lightly*, here, is *commonly* or *usually*. So in an old proverb preserved by Ray: "There's lightning *lightly* before thunder."

[133] *Too late* for *too lately*; meaning, it is too short a time since his death, not to be "to our grief, as it is yours."

YORK. I pray you, uncle, give me this dagger.

GLOUCESTER. My dagger, little cousin? with all my heart.

PRINCE. A beggar, brother?

YORK. Of my kind uncle, that I know will give;
 And being but a toy, which is no grief to give.

GLOUCESTER. A greater gift than that I'll give my cousin.

YORK. A greater gift! O, that's the sword to it.

GLOUCESTER. A gentle cousin, were it light enough.

YORK. O, then, I see, you will part but with light gifts;
 In weightier things you'll say a beggar nay.

GLOUCESTER. It is too heavy for your grace to wear.

YORK. I weigh it lightly, were it heavier.[134]

GLOUCESTER. What, would you have my weapon, little lord?

YORK. I would, that I might thank you, as—as—you call me.

GLOUCESTER. How?

YORK. Little.

PRINCE. My Lord of York will still be cross[135] in talk:
 Uncle, your grace knows how to bear with him.

YORK. You mean, to bear me, not to bear with me:—
 Uncle, my brother mocks both you and me;
 Because that I am little, like an ape,[136]
 He thinks that you should bear me on your shoulders.

BUCKINGHAM. [*Aside to* HASTINGS.] With what a sharp-provided wit he
  reasons![137]
 To mitigate the scorn he gives his uncle,
 He prettily and aptly taunts himself:
 So cunning and so young is wonderful.

GLOUCESTER. My lord, will't please you pass along?
 Myself and my good cousin Buckingham
 Will to your mother, to entreat of her
 To meet you at the Tower and welcome you.

YORK. What, will you go unto the Tower, my lord?

PRINCE. My lord protector needs will have it so.

YORK. I shall not sleep in quiet at the Tower.

---

[134] York is playing on the word *lightly*, and means, in one sense, "I hold it cheap," or "I care little for it." So in *Love's Labours Lost*, v. 2: "You *weigh* me not!—O, that's you *care not* for me."

[135] *Cross* in a logical sense, not in a moral; *opposing*, or speaking at *cross-purposes*; taking him in a wrong sense.

[136] York alludes to the hump on Gloster's back, which was commodious for carrying burdens. So in Ulpian Fulwell's *Ars Adulandi*, 1576: "Thou hast an excellent *back* to carry my lord's ape."

[137] *Provided* seems to mean *furnished, pregnant, prompt*; or it may be an instance of the passive form with an active sense, *forecasting, provident*. We have the former sense in *well-provided*, which means *well-furnished* or *well-supplied*.—Here, again, *reasons* has the sense, apparently, of *talks* or *converses*. See page 60, note 120.

GLOUCESTER. Why, what should you fear?

YORK. Marry, my uncle Clarence' angry ghost:
    My grandam told me he was murdered there.

PRINCE. I fear no uncles dead.

GLOUCESTER. Nor none that live, I hope.

PRINCE. An if they live, I hope I need not fear.
    But come, my lord; and with a heavy heart,
    Thinking on them, go I unto the Tower.

[*Sennet. Exeunt the* PRINCE, YORK, HASTINGS, CARDINAL,
    and others; *also the Lord* Mayor *and his Train.*]

BUCKINGHAM. Think you, my lord, this little prating York
    Was not incensed by his subtle mother
    To taunt and scorn you thus opprobriously?

GLOUCESTER. No doubt, no doubt; O, 'tis a parlous boy;
    Bold, quick, ingenious, forward, capable
    He is all the mother's, from the top to toe.

BUCKINGHAM. Well, let them rest.—Come hither, Catesby.
    Thou art sworn as deeply to effect what we intend
    As closely to conceal what we impart:
    Thou know'st our reasons urged upon the way;
    What think'st thou? is it not an easy matter
    To make William Lord Hastings of our mind,
    For the instalment of this noble duke
    In the seat royal of this famous isle?

CATESBY. He for his father's sake so loves the prince,
    That he will not be won to aught against him.

BUCKINGHAM. What think'st thou, then, of Stanley? what will he?

CATESBY. He will do all in all as Hastings doth.

BUCKINGHAM. Well, then, no more but this: go, gentle Catesby,
    And, as it were far off sound thou Lord Hastings,
    How doth he stand affected to our purpose;
    And summon him to-morrow to the Tower,
    To sit about the coronation.
    If thou dost find him tractable to us,
    Encourage him, and show him all our reasons:
    If he be leaden, icy-cold, unwilling,
    Be thou so too; and so break off your talk,
    And give us notice of his inclination:
    For we to-morrow hold divided councils,
    Wherein thyself shalt highly be employ'd.

GLOUCESTER. Commend me to Lord William: tell him, Catesby,
    His ancient knot of dangerous adversaries
    To-morrow are let blood at Pomfret-castle;

And bid my friend, for joy of this good news,
Give mistress Shore one gentle kiss the more.
BUCKINGHAM. Good Catesby, go, effect this business soundly.
CATESBY. My good lords both, with all the heed I may.
GLOUCESTER. Shall we hear from you, Catesby, ere we sleep?
CATESBY. You shall, my lord.
GLOUCESTER. At Crosby Place, there shall you find us both.

[*Exit* CATESBY.]

BUCKINGHAM. Now, my lord, what shall we do, if we perceive
    Lord Hastings will not yield to our complots?
GLOUCESTER. Chop off his head, man; somewhat we will do:
    And, look, when I am king, claim thou of me
    The earldom of Hereford, and the moveables
    Whereof the king my brother stood possess'd.
BUCKINGHAM. I'll claim that promise at your grace's hands.
GLOUCESTER. And look to have it yielded with all willingness.
    Come, let us sup betimes, that afterwards
    We may digest our complots in some form. [*Exeunt.*]

SCENE II.

Before Lord HASTINGS' *House.*

[*Enter a* MESSENGER.]

MESSENGER. [*Knocking.*] What, ho! my lord!
HASTINGS. [*Within.*] Who knocks at the door?
MESSENGER. A messenger from the Lord Stanley.
HASTINGS. [*Within.*] What is't o'clock?
MESSENGER. Upon the stroke of four.

[*Enter* HASTINGS.]

HASTINGS. Cannot thy master sleep these tedious nights?
MESSENGER. So it should seem by that I have to say.
    First, he commends him to your noble lordship.
HASTINGS. And then?
MESSENGER. And then he sends you word
    He dreamt to-night the boar had rased[138] his helm:

---

[138] *Rased* or *rashed* was a term commonly used to describe the violence inflicted by a boar. Nott derives it from *Arracher*, French, to *root up*, to *draw, tear*, or *pull up*. So in *The Faerie Queene*, v. 3, 8:

Besides, he says there are two councils held;
And that may be determined at the one
which may make you and him to rue at the other.
Therefore he sends to know your lordship's pleasure,
If presently you will take horse with him,
And with all speed post with him toward the north,
To shun the danger that his soul divines.

HASTINGS. Go, fellow, go, return unto thy lord;
Bid him not fear the separated councils
His honour and myself are at the one,
And at the other is my servant Catesby
Where nothing can proceed that toucheth us
Whereof I shall not have intelligence.
Tell him his fears are shallow, wanting instance:[139]
And for his dreams, I wonder he is so fond[140]
To trust the mockery of unquiet slumbers
To fly the boar before the boar pursues,
Were to incense the boar to follow us
And make pursuit where he did mean no chase.
Go, bid thy master rise and come to me
And we will both together to the Tower,
Where, he shall see, the boar[141] will use us kindly.

MESSENGER. My gracious lord, I'll tell him what you say. [*Exit.*]

[*Enter* CATESBY.]

CATESBY. Many good morrows to my noble lord!
HASTINGS. Good morrow, Catesby; you are early stirring
What news, what news, in this our tottering state?
CATESBY. It is a reeling world, indeed, my lord;
And I believe twill never stand upright
Tim Richard wear the garland of the realm.
HASTINGS. How! wear the garland! dost thou mean the crown?
CATESBY. Ay, my good lord.
HASTINGS. I'll have this crown of mine cut from my shoulders
Ere I will see the crown so foul misplaced.

There Marinell great deeds of armes did shew;
And through the thickest like a lyon flew,
Rashing off helmes, and ryving plates asonder.

[139] Without *example*, or without any matter-of-fact, to *instance*, or *allege in proof*. So in *The Merry Wives*, ii. 2, Ford says of his wife, "Now, could I come to her with any detection in my hand, my desires had *instance* and argument to commend themselves."

[140] *Fond*, here, as usual, is *foolish*, or *weak*.

[141] Of course the *boar* is Richard, whose crest was adorned with the figure of that amiable beast.

But canst thou guess that he doth aim at it?

CATESBY. Ay, on my life; and hopes to find forward
    Upon his party for the gain thereof:
    And thereupon he sends you this good news,
    That this same very day your enemies,
    The kindred of the queen, must die at Pomfret.

HASTINGS. Indeed, I am no mourner for that news,
    Because they have been still mine enemies:
    But, that I'll give my voice on Richard's side,
    To bar my master's heirs in true descent,
    God knows I will not do it, to the death.

CATESBY. God keep your lordship in that gracious mind!

HASTINGS. But I shall laugh at this a twelve-month hence,
    That they who brought me in my master's hate,
    I live to look upon their tragedy.
    Well, Catesby, ere a fortnight make me older,
    I'll send some packing that yet think not on it.

CATESBY. 'Tis a vile thing to die, my gracious lord,
    When men are unprepared and look not for it.

HASTINGS. O monstrous, monstrous! and so falls it out
    With Rivers, Vaughan, Grey: and so 'twill do
    With some men else, who think themselves as safe
    As thou and I; who, as thou know'st, are dear
    To princely Richard and to Buckingham.

CATESBY. The princes both make high account of you,—
    [*Aside.*] For they account his head upon the bridge.

HASTINGS. I know they do; and I have well deserved it.—

[*Enter* STANLEY.]

    Come on, come on; where is your boar-spear, man?
    Fear you the boar, and go so unprovided?

STANLEY. My lord, good morrow;—good morrow, Catesby:—
    You may jest on, but, by the holy Rood,[142]
    I do not like these several councils, I.

HASTINGS. My lord,
    I hold my life as dear as you do yours;
    And never in my life, I do protest,
    Was it more precious to me than 'tis now:
    Think you, but that I know our state secure,
    I would be so triumphant as I am?

STANLEY. The lords at Pomfret, when they rode from London,
    Were jocund, and supposed their state was sure,

---

[142] "The *Holy Rood*" is the *cross* or *crucifix*. A frequent oath.

And they indeed had no cause to mistrust;
But yet, you see how soon the day o'ercast.
This sudden stag of rancour I misdoubt:
Pray God, I say, I prove a needless coward![143]
What, shall we toward the Tower? the day is spent.
HASTINGS. Come, come, have with you. Wot you what, my lord?
To-day the lords you talk of are beheaded.
STANLEY. They, for their truth, might better wear their heads
Than some that have accused them wear their hats.
But come, my lord, let us away.

[*Enter a* PURSUIVANT.[144].]

HASTINGS. Go on before; I'll talk with this good fellow.

[*Exeunt* STANLEY *and* CATESBY.]

How now, sirrah! how goes the world with thee?
PURSUIVANT. The better that your lordship please to ask.
HASTINGS. I tell thee, man, 'tis better with me now
Than when I met thee last where now we meet:
Then was I going prisoner to the Tower,
By the suggestion of the queen's allies;
But now, I tell thee—keep it to thyself—
This day those enemies are put to death,
And I in better state than e'er I was.
Pursuivant. God hold it,[145] to your honour's good content!
HASTINGS. Gramercy, fellow: there, drink that for me.

[*Throws him his purse.*]

PURSUIVANT. God save your lordship! [*Exit.*]

[*Enter a* PRIEST.]

PRIEST. Well met, my lord; I am glad to see your honour.
HASTINGS. I thank thee, good Sir John, with all my heart.
I am in your debt for your last exercise;[146]

---

[143] To "prove a *needless* coward" here means, evidently, to prove a coward *needlessly* or *without cause*. Shakespeare has many instances of like construction.

[144] A *pursuivant* is now a State messenger, or one having authority to execute warrants: the word formerly meant a junior officer of the Heralds' College. In More's history this Pursuivant is spoken of as being also named Hastings.

[145] "God *hold* it" is God *continue* it.—*Gramercy*, in the next line, is *great thanks*; from the French *grand merci*.

Come the next Sabbath, and I will content you.

[*Enter* BUCKINGHAM.]

BUCKINGHAM. What, talking with a priest, lord chamberlain?
    Your friends at Pomfret, they do need the priest;
    Your honour hath no shriving-work[147] in hand.
HASTINGS. Good faith, and when I met this holy man,
    Those men you talk of came into my mind.
    What, go you toward the Tower?
BUCKINGHAM. I do, my lord; but long I shall not stay
    I shall return before your lordship thence.
HASTINGS. 'Tis like enough, for I stay dinner there.
BUCKINGHAM. [*Aside.*] And supper too, although thou know'st it
    not.—
    Come, will you go?
HASTINGS. I'll wait upon your lordship. [*Exeunt.*]

SCENE III.

Pomfret. Before the Castle.

[*Enter* RATCLIFF, *with a Guard, conducting* RIVERS, GREY,
    and VAUGHAN *to Execution.*]

RATCLIFF. Come, bring forth the prisoners.
RIVERS. Sir Richard Ratcliff, let me tell thee this:
    To-day shalt thou behold a subject die
    For truth, for duty, and for loyalty.
GREY. God keep the prince from all the pack of you!
    A knot you are of damned blood-suckers!
VAUGHAN. You live that shall cry woe for this after.
RATCLIFF. Dispatch; the limit[148] of your lives is out.
RIVERS. O Pomfret, Pomfret! O thou bloody prison,
    Fatal and ominous to noble peers!
    Within the guilty closure of thy walls
    Richard the second here was hack'd to death;
    And, for more slander to thy dismal seat,

---

[146] *Exercise* here probably means *religious instruction.*—*Sir* was in common use as a clerical title. Thus we have *Sir* Oliver Martext in *As You Like It*, and *Sir* Hugh Evans in *The Merry Wives of Windsor.*

[147] *Shriving* or *shrift* is an old word for *confession* and *absolution.*

[148] *Limit*, here, is equivalent to *appointed time*; to *appoint* being one of the old meanings of to *limit.* So in *Measure for Measure*, iii. 1: "Between which time of the contract and *limit* of the solemnity," &c.

We give thee up our guiltless blood to drink.

GREY. Now Margaret's curse is fall'n upon our heads,
For standing by when Richard stabb'd her son.

RIVERS. Then cursed she Hastings, then cursed she Buckingham,
Then cursed she Richard. O, remember, God
To hear her prayers for them, as now for us
And for my sister and her princely sons,
Be satisfied, dear God, with our true blood,
Which, as thou know'st, unjustly must be spilt.

RATCLIFF. Make haste; the hour of death is expiate.[149]

RIVERS. Come, Grey,—come, Vaughan,—let us all embrace:
And take our leave, until we meet in Heaven. [*Exeunt.*]

SCENE IV.

London. A Room in the Tower.

[BUCKINGHAM, STANLEY, HASTINGS, *the Bishop of* ELY,[150]
RATCLIFF, LOVEL, *and others, sitting at a table*; Officers *of
the Council attending.*]

HASTINGS. My lords, at once: the cause why we are met
Is, to determine of the coronation.
In God's name, speak: when is the royal day?

BUCKINGHAM. Are all things fitting for that royal time?

STANLEY. It is, and wants but nomination.[151]

BISHOP OF ELY. To-morrow, then, I judge a happy[152] day.

BUCKINGHAM. Who knows the lord protector's mind herein?
Who is most inward[153] with the royal duke?

BISHOP OF ELY. Your grace, we think, should soonest know his
mind.

BUCKINGHAM. We know each other's faces: for our hearts,
He knows no more of mine, than I of yours;

---

[149] *Expirate* for *expirated*, that is, *expired.* So, before, *convict* for *convicted.* See page 47, note 90.

[150] Dr. John Morton, who was elected to the see of Ely in 1478. He was advanced to the see of Canterbury in 1486, and appointed Lord Chancellor in 1487. He died in the year 1500. This prelate first devised the scheme of putting an end to the long contest between the Houses of York and Lancaster, by a marriage between Henry Earl of Richmond and Elizabeth, the eldest daughter of Edward IV.; and was a principal agent in bringing that arrangement about.

[151] And there wants or is wanting but a *naming of the time.*

[152] *Happy* here means *auspicious*, the same as the Latin *felix.*

[153] *Inward*, as here used, is *intimate* or *confidential.* The same word occurs as a substantive with the same sense in *Measure for Measure*, iii. 2: "Sir, I was an inward of his."

Nor I no more of his, than you of mine.—
Lord Hastings, you and he are near in love.
HASTINGS. I thank his grace, I know he loves me well;
But, for his purpose in the coronation.
I have not sounded him, nor he deliver'd
His gracious pleasure any way therein:
But you, my noble lords, may name the time;
And in the duke's behalf I'll give my voice,
Which, I presume, he'll take in gentle part.

[*Enter* GLOUCESTER.]

BISHOP OF ELY. Now in good time, here comes the duke himself.
GLOUCESTER. My noble lords and cousins all, good morrow.
I have been long a sleeper; but, I hope,
My absence doth neglect no great designs,
Which by my presence might have been concluded.
BUCKINGHAM. Had not you come upon your cue,[154] my lord
William Lord Hastings had pronounced your part,—
I mean, your voice,—for crowning of the king.
GLOUCESTER. Than my Lord Hastings no man might be bolder;
His lordship knows me well, and loves me well.
HASTINGS. I thank your grace.
GLOUCESTER. My lord of Ely!
BISHOP OF ELY. My lord?
GLOUCESTER. When I was last in Holborn,
I saw good strawberries in your garden there
I do beseech you send for some of them.[155]
BISHOP OF ELY. Marry, and will, my lord, with all my heart. [*Exit.*]
GLOUCESTER. Cousin of Buckingham, a word with you.

[*Takes him aside.*]

Catesby hath sounded Hastings in our business,

---

[154] An expression borrowed from the stage: the *cue, queue,* or *tail* of a speech being the last words, and so indicating to the next speaker when to *take his turn.*

[155] This easy affability and smoothness of humour when going about the blackest and bloodiest crimes is one of the most telling strokes in this terrible portrait. The incident is thus related in the History: "These lords so sitting togither communing of this matter, the protector came in amongst them first about nine of the clocke, saluting them courteouslie, and excusing himselfe that had been from them so long, saieng merilie that he had beene a sleeper that daie. After a little talking with them he said unto the bishop of Elie, My lord, you have verie good strawberies at your garden in Holborne; I require you, let us have a messe of them. Gladlie, my lord, quoth he; would God I had some better thing as readie to your pleasure as that! And therewithall in all hast he sent his servant for a messe of strawberies."

And finds the testy gentleman so hot,
As he will lose his head ere give consent
His master's son, as worshipful as he terms it,
Shall lose the royalty of England's throne.
BUCKINGHAM. Withdraw you hence, my lord, I'll follow you.

[*Exit* GLOUCESTER, *followed by* BUCKINGHAM.]

STANLEY. We have not yet set down this day of triumph.
To-morrow, in mine opinion, is too sudden;
For I myself am not so well provided
As else I would be, were the day prolong'd.

[*Re-enter the Bishop of* ELY.]

BISHOP OF ELY. Where is my lord protector? I have sent for these
strawberries.
HASTINGS. His grace looks cheerfully and smooth to-day;
There's some conceit or other likes[156] him well,
When he doth bid good morrow with such a spirit.
I think there's never a man in Christendom
That can less hide his love or hate than he;
For by his face straight shall you know his heart.
STANLEY. What of his heart perceive you in his face
By any likelihood he show'd to-day?
HASTINGS. Marry, that with no man here he is offended;
For, were he, he had shown it in his looks.
STANLEY. I pray God he be not, I say.

[*Re-enter* GLOUCESTER *and* BUCKINGHAM.]

GLOUCESTER. I pray you all, tell me what they deserve
That do conspire my death with devilish plots
Of damned witchcraft, and that have prevail'd
Upon my body with their hellish charms?
HASTINGS. The tender love I bear your grace, my lord,
Makes me most forward in this noble presence
To doom the offenders, whatsoever they be
I say, my lord, they have deserved death.
GLOUCESTER. Then be your eyes the witness of this ill:
See how I am bewitch'd; behold mine arm
Is, like a blasted sapling, wither'd up:

---

[156] Some *thought* or *conception* that *pleases* him well. *Conceit* is generally so in old
writers, and *likes* very often so.

And this is Edward's wife, that monstrous witch,
Consorted with that harlot strumpet Shore,
That by their witchcraft thus have marked me.
HASTINGS. If they have done this thing, my gracious lord,—
GLOUCESTER. If I thou protector of this damned strumpet,
  Tellest thou me of *ifs*? Thou art a traitor:—
  Off with his head! Now, by Saint Paul I swear,
  I will not dine until I see the same.—
  Lovel and Ratcliff,[157] look that it be done:—
  The rest, that love me, rise and follow me.

[*Exeunt all but* HASTINGS, LOVEL, *and* RATCLIFF.]

HASTINGS. Woe, woe for England! not a whit for me;
  For I, too fond, might have prevented this.
  Stanley did dream the boar did raze his helm;
  But I disdain'd it, and did scorn to fly:
  Three times to-day my foot-cloth horse[158] did stumble,
  And startled, when he look'd upon the Tower,
  As loath to bear me to the slaughter-house.
  O, now I want the priest that spake to me:
  I now repent I told the pursuivant
  As 'twere triumphing at mine enemies,
  How they at Pomfret bloodily were butcher'd,
  And I myself secure in grace and favour.—
  O Margaret, Margaret, now thy heavy curse
  Is lighted on poor Hastings' wretched head!
RATCLIFF. Dispatch, my lord; the duke would be at dinner:
  Make a short shrift; he longs to see your head.
HASTINGS. O momentary grace of mortal men,
  Which we more hunt for than the grace of God!
  Who builds his hopes in air of your good looks,
  Lives like a drunken sailor on a mast,
  Ready, with every nod, to tumble down
  Into the fatal bowels of the deep.
LOVEL. Come, come, dispatch; 'tis bootless to exclaim.

---

[157] In the preceding scene, we have Ratcliff at Pomfret, conducting Rivers, Grey, and Vaughan to death; yet the events of that scene and this are represented as occurring the same day. Knight thinks "this is one of those positions in which the Poet has trusted to the imagination of his audience rather than to their topographical knowledge." It may be so, but it seems to me much more likely to have been a simple oversight on the Poet's part.

[158] A *foot-cloth* was a kind of housing that covered the body of the horse, and reached nearly to the ground. A *foot-cloth* horse was a palfrey covered with such housings, used for state; and was the usual mode of conveyance for the rich, at a period when carriages were unknown.

HASTINGS. O bloody Richard!—miserable England!
    I prophesy the fearful'st time to thee
    That ever wretched age hath look'd upon.
    Come, lead me to the block; bear him my head.
    They smile at me that shortly shall be dead.[159] [*Exeunt.*]

SCENE V.

The Same. The Tower-walls.

[*Enter* GLOUCESTER *and* BUCKINGHAM, *in rusty armour,
    marvellous ill-favoured.*]

GLOUCESTER. Come, cousin, canst thou quake, and change thy
        colour,
    Murder thy breath in the middle of a word,
    And then begin again, and stop again,
    As if thou wert distraught[160] and mad with terror?
BUCKINGHAM. Tut, I can counterfeit the deep tragedian;
    Speak and look back, and pry on every side,
    Tremble and start at wagging of a straw,
    Intending[161] deep suspicion: ghastly looks
    Are at my service, like enforced smiles;
    And both are ready in their offices,
    At any time, to grace my stratagems.
    But what, is Catesby gone?
GLOUCESTER. He is; and, see, he brings the mayor along.
BUCKINGHAM. Let me alone to entertain him.—

[*Enter the Lord* Mayor *and* CATESBY.]

    Lord mayor,—
GLOUCESTER. Look to the drawbridge there!
BUCKINGHAM. Hark! a drum.
GLOUCESTER. Catesby, o'erlook the walls.
BUCKINGHAM. Lord mayor, the reason we have sent—
GLOUCESTER. Look back, defend thee, here are enemies.

---

[159] William Lord Hastings was beheaded on the 13th of June, 1483. His eldest son by Catharine Neville, daughter of Richard Neville, Earl of Salisbury, and widow of William Lord Bonville, was restored to his honours and estate by King Henry VII. in the first year of his reign.

[160] *Distraught* is an old form of *distracted.*

[161] *Intend* is repeatedly used by Shakespeare for *pretend.* So, again, in the seventh scene of this Act: "*Intend* some fear." Also, in *Lucrece*: "For then is Tarquin brought unto his bed, intending weariness with heavy sprite." On the other hand, the Poet repeatedly has *pretend* and its derivatives in the sense of *intend.*

BUCKINGHAM. God and our innocence defend and guard us!
GLOUCESTER. Be patient, they are friends, Ratcliff and Lovel.

[*Enter* LOVEL *and* RATCLIFF, *with* HASTINGS' *head.*]

LOVEL. Here is the head of that ignoble traitor,
  The dangerous and unsuspected Hastings.
GLOUCESTER. So dear I loved the man, that I must weep.
  I took him for the plainest harmless creature
  That breathed upon this earth a Christian;
  Made him my book wherein my soul recorded
  The history of all her secret thoughts:
  So smooth he daub'd[162] his vice with show of virtue,
  That, his apparent open guilt omitted,—
  I mean, his conversation[163] with Shore's wife,—
  He lived from all attainder of suspect.[164]
BUCKINGHAM. Well, well, he was the covert'st shelter'd traitor
  That ever lived.—
  Would you imagine, or almost believe,—
  Were't not that, by great preservation,
  We live to tell it you,—the subtle traitor
  This day had plotted, in the Council-house
  To murder me and my good Lord of Gloucester?
LORD MAYOR. What, had he so?
GLOUCESTER. What, think You we are Turks or infidels?
  Or that we would, against the form of law,
  Proceed thus rashly to the villain's death,
  But that the extreme peril of the case,
  The peace of England and our persons' safety,
  Enforced us to this execution?
LORD MAYOR. Now, fair befall you! he deserved his death;
  And you my good lords, both have well proceeded,
  To warn false traitors from the like attempts.
  I never look'd for better at his hands,
  After he once fell in with Mistress Shore.
GLOUCESTER. Yet had not we determined he should die,
  Until your lordship came to see his death;
  Which now the loving haste of these our friends,
  Somewhat against our meaning, have[165] prevented;

---

[162] To *daub* was used for to *disguise*, to *cover over.* So in *King Lear*, iv. 1 : "I cannot *daub* it further."

[163] Familiar intercourse; what is now called *criminal conversation.—Apparent*, again, in the sense of *manifest.* See page 58, note 113.

[164] *Suspect* for *suspicion.* So, before, in i. 3: "You do me shameful injury, falsely to draw me in these vile *suspects.*"

Because, my lord, we would have had you heard
The traitor speak, and timorously confess
The manner and the purpose of his treason;
That you might well have signified the same
Unto the citizens, who haply may
Misconstrue us in him and wail his death.
LORD MAYOR. But, my good lord, your grace's word shall serve,
As well as I had seen and heard him speak
And doubt you not, right noble princes both,
But I'll acquaint our duteous citizens
With all your just proceedings in this cause.
GLOUCESTER. And to that end we wish'd your lord-ship here,
To avoid the carping censures of the world.
BUCKINGHAM. But since you come too late of[166] our intents,
Yet witness what you hear we did intend:
And so, my good lord mayor, we bid farewell.

[*Exit Lord* MAYOR.]

GLOUCESTER. Go, after, after, cousin Buckingham.
The mayor towards Guildhall hies him in all post:
There, at your meet'st advantage of the time,
Infer[167] the bastardy of Edward's children:
Tell them how Edward put to death a citizen,
Only for saying he would make his son
Heir to the crown; meaning indeed his house,
Which, by the sign thereof was termed so.[168]
Moreover, urge his hateful luxury
And bestial appetite in change of lust;
Which stretched to their servants, daughters, wives,
Even where his lustful eye or savage heart,
Without control, listed to make his prey.
Nay, for a need, thus far come near my person:
Tell them, when that my mother went with child
Of that insatiate Edward, noble York
My princely father then had wars in France

---

[165] Properly it should be *has*. But the old writers have many such instances where the verb is made to agree with the nearest substantive, as with *friends* here, instead of its proper subject.

[166] In common speech a similar phrase is used, "to come *short of* a thing."

[167] *Infer* is here used in the sense of *introduce* or *bring forward*; one of its Latin senses. So in iv. 4, of this play: "infer fair England's peace by this alliance."

[168] This person was one *Walker*, a substantial citizen and grocer, at the Crown in Cheapside. These topics of Edward's cruelty, lust, unlawful marriage, &c., are enlarged upon in that most extraordinary invective, the petition presented to Richard before his accession, which was afterwards turned into an Act of Parliament.

And, by just computation of the time,
Found that the issue was not his begot;
Which well appeared in his lineaments,
Being nothing like the noble duke my father:
But touch this sparingly, as 'twere far off,
Because you know, my lord, my mother lives.

BUCKINGHAM. Fear not, my lord, I'll play the orator
As if the golden fee for which I plead
Were for myself: and so, my lord, adieu.

GLOUCESTER. If you thrive well, bring them to Baynard's Castle;[169]
Where you shall find me well accompanied
With reverend fathers and well-learned bishops.

BUCKINGHAM. I go: and towards three or four o'clock
Look for the news that the Guildhall affords. [*Exit.*]

GLOUCESTER. Go, Lovel, with all speed to Doctor Shaw,—
[*To* CATESBY.] Go thou to Friar Penker:[170]—bid them both
Meet me within this hour at Baynard's Castle.—

[*Exeunt* LOVEL, CATESBY, *and* RATCLIFF.]

Now will I in, to take some privy order,
To draw the brats of Clarence out of sight;
And to give notice, that no manner of person[171]
At any time have recourse unto the princes. [*Exit.*]

SCENE VI.

The Same. A Street.

[*Enter a* SCRIVENER.[172]]

SCRIVENER. This is the indictment of the good Lord Hastings;
Which in a set hand fairly is engross'd,[173]

---

[169] This castle was built by Baynard, a nobleman who is said to have come in with William the Conqueror. It stood on the bank of the river in Thames-street, but has been swept away by the commercial necessities of London.

[170] Dr. Shaw was brother to the Lord Mayor; Penker, according to Speed, was provincial of the Augustine friars; and both were popular preachers of the time.

[171] The expression "no manner person" is according to the idiom of the time.—"The brats of Clarence" were Edward and Margaret, known afterwards as Earl of Warwick and Countess of Salisbury.

[172] A *scrivener* is, literally, a *writer* or a *scribe*. The term was applied to a class of men whose special business it was to draw up or to transcribe legal writings and instruments.

[173] To *engross*, as the word is here used, is to copy legal or other documents in a clear, legible hand for public use.—In the olden time, St. Paul's Cathedral was used as a sort of exchange, and all sorts of notices were posted there for the public eye. The edifice

That it may be this day read over in Paul's.
And mark how well the sequel hangs together:
Eleven hours I spent to write it over,
For yesternight by Catesby was it brought me;
The precedent[174] was full as long a-doing:
And yet within these five hours lived Lord Hastings,
Untainted, unexamined, free, at liberty
Here's a good world the while! Why who's so gross,
That seeth not this palpable device?
Yet who's so blind, but says he sees it not?
Bad is the world; and all will come to nought,
When such bad dealings must be seen in thought.[175] [*Exit.*]

SCENE VII.

The Same. Court of Baynard's Castle.

[*Enter* GLOUCESTER *and* BUCKINGHAM, *meeting.*]

GLOUCESTER. How now, my lord, what say the citizens?
BUCKINGHAM. Now, by the holy mother of our Lord,
　　The citizens are mum and speak not a word.
GLOUCESTER. Touch'd you the bastardy of Edward's children?
BUCKINGHAM. I did; with his contract with Lady Lucy,[176]
　　And his contract by deputy in France;
　　The insatiate greediness of his desires,
　　And his enforcement of the city wives;
　　His tyranny for trifles; his own bastardy,[177]
　　As being got, your father then in France,

---

was not used in Shakespeare's time, it having been set on fire by a stroke of lightning and the roof burnt off early in Elizabeth's reign. The present St. Paul's was not built till the time of Charles the Second.

[174] The original draft from which the copy was made.

[175] "Seen in *thought* is seen in *silence.*"—I am not certain whether the last word of the preceding line should be *nought* or *naught*. With the latter, the sense is about the same as in our phrase of "going to the *bad.*" See page 21, note 17.

[176] The King had been familiar with this lady before his marriage with the present Queen, to obstruct which his mother alleged a precontract between them. But Elizabeth Lucy, being sworn to speak the truth, declared that the King had not been affianced to her. Edward, however, had been married to Lady Eleanor Butler, widow of Lord Butler of Sudley, and daughter to the great Earl of Shrewsbury. On this ground his children were declared illegitimate by the only Parliament convened by Richard; but nothing was said of Elizabeth Lucy.

[177] This tale is supposed to have been first propagated by the Duke of Clarence when he obtained a settlement of the crown on himself and his issue after the death of Henry VI. Sir Thomas More says that the Duke of Gloster, soon after Edward's death, revived this scandal.

His resemblance, being not like the duke;
Withal I did infer[178] your lineaments,
Being the right idea[179] of your father,
Both in your form and nobleness of mind;
Laid open all your victories in Scotland,
Your discipline in war, wisdom in peace,
Your bounty, virtue, fair humility:
Indeed, left nothing fitting for the purpose
Untouch'd, or slightly handled, in discourse
And when mine oratory grew to an end
I bid them that did love their country's good
Cry, *God save Richard, England's royal king*!

GLOUCESTER. Ah! and did they so?

BUCKINGHAM. No, so God help me, they spake not a word;
But, like dumb statuas[180] or breathing stones,
Gazed each on other, and look'd deadly pale.
Which when I saw, I reprehended them;
And ask'd the mayor what meant this wilful silence:
His answer was, the people were not wont
To be spoke to but by the recorder.
Then he was urged to tell my tale again,
Thus saith the duke, thus hath the duke inferr'd;
But nothing spake in warrant from himself.
When he had done, some followers of mine own,
At the lower end of the hall, hurl'd up their caps,
And some ten voices cried *God save King Richard*!
And thus I took the vantage of those few,
Thanks, gentle citizens and friends, quoth I;
This general applause and loving shout
Argues your wisdoms and your love to Richard:
And even here brake off, and came away.

GLOUCESTER. What tongueless blocks were they! would not they
speak?

BUCKINGHAM. No, by my troth, my lord.

GLOUCESTER. Will not the mayor then and his brethren come?

BUCKINGHAM. The mayor is here at hand: intend some fear;
Be not you spoke with, but by mighty suit:
And look you get a prayer-book in your hand,
And stand betwixt two churchmen,[181] good my lord;
For on that ground I'll build a holy descant:[182]

---

[178] *Infer* again as explained in note 167, page 80.
[179] *Idea* is here used in the right classic sense of *image* or *likeness*.
[180] *Statue* was very often written and printed *statua*, as a trisyllable.
[181] *Churchmen* was formerly used of what are now called clergymen.

And be not easily won to our request:
Play the maid's part, still answer nay, and take it.
GLOUCESTER. I go; and if you plead as well for them
  As I can say nay to thee for myself,
  No doubt well bring it to a happy issue.
BUCKINGHAM. Go, go, up to the leads;[183] the lord mayor knocks.—

[*Exit* GLOUCESTER.]

[*Enter the Lord* Mayor, Aldermen, *and* Citizens.]

Welcome my lord; I dance attendance here;
I think the duke will not be spoke withal.—

[*Enter, from the Castle*, CATESBY.]

Here comes his servant: how now, Catesby,
What says he?
CATESBY. My lord: he doth entreat your grace;
  To visit him to-morrow or next day:
  He is within, with two right reverend fathers,
  Divinely bent to meditation;
  And no worldly suit would he be moved,
  To draw him from his holy exercise.
BUCKINGHAM. Return, good Catesby, to thy lord again;
  Tell him, myself, the mayor and citizens,
  In deep designs and matters of great moment,
  No less importing than our general good,
  Are come to have some conference with his grace.
CATESBY. I'll tell him what you say, my lord. [*Exit.*]
BUCKINGHAM. Ah, ha, my lord, this prince is not an Edward!
  He is not lolling on a lewd day-bed,
  But on his knees at meditation;
  Not dallying with a brace of courtesans,
  But meditating with two deep divines;
  Not sleeping, to engross[184] his idle body,
  But praying, to enrich his watchful soul:
  Happy were England, would this gracious prince
  Take on himself the sovereignty thereof:
  But, sure, I fear, we shall ne'er win him to it.

---

[182] *Ground* and *descant* were technical terms in music; the former meaning the original air, the latter the variations.

[183] Formerly many buildings were roofed with lead. "Up to the *leads*" therefore means up to the *roof*, or close under the *eaves*; the topmost part of the building.

[184] That is, to pamper, fatten, or *make gross.*

LORD MAYOR. Marry, God forbid his grace should say us nay!
BUCKINGHAM. I fear he will. Here Catesby comes again.—

[*Re-enter* CATESBY.]

 Now, Catesby, what says his Grace?
CATESBY. He wonders to what end you have assembled
 Such troops of citizens to speak with him,
 His grace not being warn'd thereof before:
 My lord, he fears you mean no good to him.
BUCKINGHAM. Sorry I am my noble cousin should
 Suspect me, that I mean no good to him:
 By heaven, I come in perfect love to him;
 And so once more return and tell his Grace.—

[*Exit* CATESBY.]

 When holy and devout religious men
 Are at their beads, 'tis hard to draw them thence,
 So sweet is zealous contemplation.

[*Enter* GLOUCESTER *in a gallery above, between two* Bishops.
CATESBY *returns.*]

LORD MAYOR. See, where he stands between two clergymen!
BUCKINGHAM. Two props of virtue for a Christian prince,
 To stay him from the fall of vanity:
 And, see, a book of prayer[185] in his hand,—
 True ornaments to know a holy man.—
 Famous Plantagenet, most gracious prince,
 Lend favourable ears to our request;
 And pardon us the interruption
 Of thy devotion and right Christian zeal.
GLOUCESTER. My lord, there needs no such apology:
 I rather do beseech you pardon me,
 Who, earnest in the service of my God,
 Neglect the visitation of my friends.
 But, leaving this, what is your grace's pleasure?
BUCKINGHAM. Even that, I hope, which pleaseth God above,
 And all good men of this ungovern'd isle.
GLOUCESTER. I do suspect I have done some offence

---

[185] *Prayer* is used by Shakespeare as one or two syllables indifferently, to suit his verse. Here it is a dissyllable. The same of *hour, fire, even, given, power, flower, toward* or *towards,* and sundry others.

That seems disgracious in the city's eyes,
And that you come to reprehend my ignorance.
BUCKINGHAM. You have, my lord: would it might please your
    grace,
At our entreaties, to amend that fault!
GLOUCESTER. Else wherefore breathe I in a Christian land?
BUCKINGHAM. Then know, it is your fault that you resign
    The supreme seat, the throne majestical,
    The scepter'd office of your ancestors,
    Your state of fortune and your due of birth,
    The lineal glory of your royal house,
    To the corruption of a blemished stock:
    Whilst, in the mildness of your sleepy thoughts,—
    Which here we waken to our country's good,—
    This noble isle doth want her proper limbs;
    Her face defaced with scars of infamy,
    Her royal stock graft with ignoble plants,
    And almost shoulder'd in[186] the swallowing gulf
    Of blind forgetfulness and dark oblivion.
    Which to recure,[187] we heartily solicit
    Your gracious self to take on you the charge
    And kingly government of this your land,
    Not as protector, steward, substitute,
    Or lowly factor for another's gain;
    But as successively from blood to blood,
    Your right of birth, your empery, your own.
    For this, consorted with the citizens,
    Your very worshipful and loving friends,
    And by their vehement instigation,
    In this just suit come I to move your grace.
GLOUCESTER. I know not whether to depart in silence,
    Or bitterly to speak in your reproof.
    Best fitteth my degree or your condition
    If not to answer, you might haply think
    Tongue-tied ambition, not replying, yielded

---

[186] *In* for *into*, the two being often used indiscriminately.—To *shoulder*, as the word
is here used, is to *thrust* or *heave* by force or violence. Steevens quotes a similar
expression from Lyson's *Environs of London*: "Lyke tyraunts and lyke madde men
helpynge to *shulderynge* other of the sayd bannermen ynto the dyche."—In the preceding
line, *graft* for *grafted*, as before *convict* for *convicted*. See page 47, note 90.
[187] To *recure* is to *recover*. Spenser has the word repeatedly in the same sense. So
The Faerie Queene, ii. 12, 19:

    Whose mariners and merchants with much toyle
    Labour'd in vaine to have *recur'd* their prize.

To bear the golden yoke of sovereignty,
Which fondly you would here impose on me;
If to reprove you for this suit of yours,
So season'd with your faithful love to me.
Then, on the other side, I cheque'd my friends.
Therefore,—to speak, and to avoid the first,
And then, in speaking, not to incur the last,—
Definitively thus I answer you.
Your love deserves my thanks; but my desert
Unmeritable[188] shuns your high request.
First if all obstacles were cut away,
And that my path were even to the crown,
As my ripe revenue and due by birth
Yet so much is my poverty of spirit,
So mighty and so many my defects,
As I had rather hide me from my greatness—
Being a bark to brook no mighty sea—
Than in my greatness covet to be hid,
And in the vapour of my glory smother'd.
But, God be thank'd, there's no need of me,
And much I need to help you, were there need:[189]
The royal tree hath left us royal fruit,
Which, mellow'd by the stealing hours of time,
Will well become the seat of majesty,
And make, no doubt, us happy by his reign.
On him I lay what you would lay on me,
The right and fortune of his happy stars;
Which God defend[190] that I should wring from him!
BUCKINGHAM. My lord, this argues conscience in your grace;
But the respects thereof are nice[191] and trivial,
All circumstances well considered.
You say that Edward is your brother's son:
So say we too, but not by Edward's wife;
For first he was contract to Lady Lucy,—
Your mother lives a witness to that vow,—
And afterward by substitute betroth'd
To Bona, sister to the King of France.
These both put by a poor petitioner,

---

[188] *Unmeritable* for *unmeriting*. This indiscriminate use of active and passive forms has been repeatedly noted.

[189] "And I fall far short of the ability to help you, if help were needed."

[190] "God *defend*" is the same as God *forbid*. Repeatedly used thus by Shakespeare; and a common usage of the time.

[191] *Respects* for *considerations*; a frequent sense of the word.—*Nice* here means *unimportant*, or, perhaps, *over-scrupulous*.

A care-crazed mother of a many children,
A beauty-waning and distressed widow,
Even in the afternoon of her best days,
Made prize and purchase of his lustful eye,
Seduced the pitch and height of all his thoughts
To base declension and loathed bigamy
By her, in his unlawful bed, he got
This Edward, whom our manners term the prince.
More bitterly could I expostulate,
Save that, for reverence to some alive,[192]
I give a sparing limit to my tongue.
Then, good my lord, take to your royal self
This proffer'd benefit of dignity;
If non to bless us and the land withal,
Yet to draw forth your noble ancestry
From the corruption of abusing times,
Unto a lineal true-derived course.

LORD MAYOR. Do, good my lord, your citizens entreat you.

BUCKINGHAM. Refuse not, mighty lord, this proffer'd love.

CATESBY. O, make them joyful, grant their lawful suit!

GLOUCESTER. Alas, why would you heap these cares on me?
I am unfit for state and majesty;
I do beseech you, take it not amiss;
I cannot nor I will not yield to you.

BUCKINGHAM. If you refuse it,—as, in love and zeal,
Loath to depose the child, Your brother's son;
As well we know your tenderness of heart
And gentle, kind, effeminate remorse,[193]
Which we have noted in you to your kin,
And equally indeed to all estates,—
Yet whether you accept our suit or no,
Your brother's son shall never reign our king;
But we will plant some other in the throne,
To the disgrace and downfall of your house:
And in this resolution here we leave you.—
Come, citizens: 'zounds! I'll entreat no more.

GLOUCESTER. O, do not swear, my Lord of Buckingham.

[*Exit* BUCKINGHAM, *the* Mayor, Aldermen *and* Citizens
    retiring.]

---

[192] Buckingham here hints at the pretended illegitimacy of Edward and Clarence. By "some alive" he means the Duchess of York, the mother of Edward and Richard. See near the close of scene 5, "Nay, for a need, thus far come near my person," &c.

[193] *Remorse*, again, for *pity* or *compassion*. See page 28, note 40.

CATESBY. Call them again, my lord, and accept their suit.
ANOTHER. Do, good my lord, lest all the land do rue it.
GLOUCESTER. Would you enforce me to a world of care?
 Call them again.

[CATESBY *goes to the* Mayor, *&c., and then exit.*]

 —I am not made of stone,
But penetrable to your. kind entreats,
Albeit against my conscience and my soul.

[*Re-enter* BUCKINGHAM *and* CATESBY; *the* Mayor, *&c.,*
 coming forward.]

Cousin of Buckingham,—and you sage, grave men,—
Since you will buckle fortune on my back,
To bear her burthen, whether I will or no,
I must have patience to endure the load:
But if black scandal or foul-faced reproach
Attend the sequel of your imposition,
Your mere enforcement shall acquittance[194] me
From all the impure blots and stains thereof;
For God he knows, and you may partly see,
How far I am from the desire thereof.
LORD MAYOR. God bless your grace! we see it, and will say it.
GLOUCESTER. In saying so, you shall but say the truth.
BUCKINGHAM. Then I salute you with this kingly title:
 Long live Richard, England's royal king!
LORD MAYOR and CITIZENS. Amen.
BUCKINGHAM. To-morrow will it please you to be crown'd?
GLOUCESTER. Even when you please, since you will have it so.
BUCKINGHAM. To-morrow, then, we will attend your grace:
 And so most joyfully we take our leave.
GLOUCESTER. [*To the* Bishops.] Come, let us to our holy task
  again.—
 Farewell, good cousin;—farewell, gentle friends. [*Exeunt.*]

---

[194] *Acquittance* for *acquit*, because the verse wanted a trisyllable.

ACT IV.

SCENE I.

London. Before the Tower.

[*Enter, on one side, Queen* ELIZABETH, *Duchess of* YORK, *and*
        DORSET;   *on   the   other,*   ANNE,   *Duchess   of*
        GLOUCESTER,[195]   *leading   Lady*   MARGARET
        PLANTAGENET, CLARENCE's *young Daughter.*]

DUCHESS OF YORK. Who meets us here? my niece[196] Plantagenet
Led in the hand of her kind aunt of Gloucester?
Now, for my life, she's wandering to the Tower,
On pure heart's love to greet the tender Princes.—
Daughter, well met.
LADY ANNE. God give your graces both
A happy and a joyful time of day!
QUEEN ELIZABETH. As much to you, good sister! Whither away?
LADY ANNE. No farther than the Tower; and, as I guess,
Upon the like devotion as yourselves,
To gratulate the gentle Princes there.
QUEEN ELIZABETH. Kind sister, thanks: we'll enter all together.
And, in good time, here the lieutenant comes.—

[*Enter* BRAKENBURY.]

Master lieutenant, pray you, by your leave,
How doth the prince, and my young son of York?
BRAKENBURY. Right well, dear madam. By your patience,
I may not suffer you to visit them;
The king hath straitly charged the contrary.
QUEEN ELIZABETH. The king! why, who's that?
BRAKENBURY. I cry you mercy: I mean the lord protector.
QUEEN ELIZABETH. The Lord protect him from that kingly title!
Hath he set bounds betwixt their love and me?
I am their mother; who should keep me from them?
DUCHESS OF YORK. I am their fathers mother; I will see them.
LADY ANNE. Their aunt I am in law, in love their mother:

---

[195] We have not seen this lady since the second scene of the first Act, in which she promised to meet Richard at Crosby-place. She was married to him about the year 1472.

[196] The Duchess is speaking to what we should call her grand-daughter. But the words *grand-son, grand-daughter, grand-children,* are not used by Shakespeare at all; their places being supplied by *nephew* and *niece*; sometimes by *cousin.*

Then bring me to their sights; I'll bear thy blame
And take thy office from thee, on my peril.
BRAKENBURY. No, madam, no; I may not leave it so:[197]
I am bound by oath, and therefore pardon me. [*Exit.*]

[*Enter* STANLEY.]

STANLEY. Let me but meet you, ladies, one hour hence,
And I'll salute your grace of York as mother,
And reverend looker on, of two fair queens.—
[*To* ANNE.] Come, madam, you must straight to Westminster,
There to be crowned Richard's royal queen.
QUEEN ELIZABETH. O, cut my lace in sunder, that my pent heart
May have some scope to beat, or else I swoon
With this dead-killing news!
LADY ANNE. Despiteful tidings! O unpleasing news!
DORSET. Be of good cheer:—mother, how fares your grace?
QUEEN ELIZABETH. O Dorset, speak not to me, get thee hence!
Death and destruction dog thee at the heels;
Thy mother's name is ominous to children.
If thou wilt outstrip death, go cross the seas,
And live with Richmond, from the reach of hell
Go, hie thee, hie thee from this slaughter-house,
Lest thou increase the number of the dead;
And make me die the thrall of Margaret's curse,
Nor mother, wife, nor England's counted queen.
STANLEY. Full of wise care is this your counsel, madam.—
Take all the swift advantage of the hours;
You shall have letters from me to my son
To meet you on the way, and welcome you.
Be not ta'en tardy by unwise delay.
DUCHESS OF YORK. O ill-dispersing wind of misery!—
O my accursed womb, the bed of death!
A cockatrice[198] hast thou hatch'd to the world,
Whose unavoided eye is murderous.
STANLEY. Come, madam, come; I in all haste was sent.
LADY ANNE. And I in all unwillingness will go.

---

[197] He refers to his office or charge, which she has offered to take upon herself at her own risk or peril.

[198] The *cockatrice* was so called from its fabled generation from the egg of a cock; the term being derived from *cock* and *atter*, Anglo-Saxon for *adder*. *Cockatrice*, it seems, was but another name for the *basilisk*. So in Browne's *Vulgar Errors*, Book iii. chap. 7: "Many opinions are passant concerning the basilisk, or little king of serpents, commonly called the *cockatrice*." And again: "As for the generation of the *basilisk*, that it proceedeth from a *cock's egg*, hatched under a toad or serpent, it is a conceit as monstrous as the brood itself." See page 27, note 39.

I would to God that the inclusive verge
Of golden metal that must round my brow
Were red-hot steel, to sear me to the brain![199]
Anointed let me be with deadly venom,
And die, ere men can say, *God save the Queen*!

QUEEN ELIZABETH. Go, go, poor soul, I envy not thy glory
    To feed my humour, wish thyself no harm.

LADY ANNE. No! why? When he that is my husband now
    Came to me, as I follow'd Henry's corpse,
    When scarce the blood was well wash'd from his hands
    Which issued from my other angel husband
    And that dead saint which then I weeping follow'd;
    O, when, I say, I look'd on Richard's face,
    This was my wish: *Be thou*, quoth I, *accursed*,
    For making me, so young, so old a widow!
    And, when thou wed'st, let sorrow haunt thy bed;
    And be thy wife—if any be so mad—
    As miserable by the life of thee
    As thou hast made me by my dear lord's death!
    Lo, ere I can repeat this curse again,
    Even in so short a space, my woman's heart
    Grossly grew captive to his honey words
    And proved the subject of my own soul's curse,
    Which ever since hath kept my eyes from rest;
    For never yet one hour in his bed
    Have I enjoy'd the golden dew of sleep,
    But have been waked by his timorous dreams.[200]
    Besides, he hates me for my father Warwick;
    And will, no doubt, shortly be rid of me.

QUEEN ELIZABETH. Poor heart, adieu! I pity thy complaining.

LADY ANNE. No more than from my soul I mourn for yours.

QUEEN ELIZABETH. Farewell, thou woful welcomer of glory!

LADY ANNE. Adieu, poor soul, that takest thy leave of it!

DUCHESS OF YORK. [*To* DORSET.] Go thou to Richmond, and
    good fortune guide thee!—

---

[199] She seems to allude to the ancient mode of punishing a regicide, or other criminals, by placing a crown of iron heated red-hot upon his head. In some of the monkish accounts of a place of future torments, a *burning crown* is likewise appropriated to those who deprived any lawful monarch of his kingdom. The Earl of Athol, who was executed for the murder of James I., King of Scots, was previous to death crowned with a hot iron.

[200] This is from the History: "He tooke ill rest a nights, laie long waking and musing, sore wearied with care and watch, rather slumbered than slept, *troubled with fearfull dreames*, suddenlie sometime start up, lept out of his bed, and ran about the chamber; so was his restless heart continuallie tossed and tumbled with the tedious impression and stormie remembrance of his abhominable deed."

[*To* ANNE.] Go thou to Richard, and good angels guard thee!—
[*To* ELIZABETH.] Go thou to sanctuary, and good thoughts possess
    thee!—
I to my grave, where peace and rest lie with me!
Eighty odd years[201] of sorrow have I seen,
And each hour's joy wrecked with a week of teen.[202]
QUEEN ELIZABETH. Stay, yet look back with me unto the Tower.—
    Pity, you ancient stones, those tender babes
    Whom envy hath immured within your walls!
    Rough cradle for such little pretty ones!
    Rude ragged nurse, old sullen playfellow
    For tender princes, use my babies well!
    So foolish sorrow bids your stones farewell. [*Exeunt.*]

SCENE II.

The Same. A Room of State in the Palace.

[*Sennet. Enter King* RICHARD III, *crowned*; BUCKINGHAM,
    CATESBY, *a* PAGE, *and others.*]

KING RICHARD III. Stand all apart.—Cousin of Buckingham,—
BUCKINGHAM. My gracious sovereign?
KING RICHARD III. Give me thy hand. [*Ascends the throne.*] Thus
    high, by thy advice
    And thy assistance, is King Richard seated;
    But shall we wear these honours for a day?
    Or shall they last, and we rejoice in them?
BUCKINGHAM. Still live they and for ever may they last!
KING RICHARD III. O Buckingham, now do I play the touch,[203]
    To try if thou be current gold indeed
    Young Edward lives: think now what I would say.
BUCKINGHAM. Say on, my loving lord.
KING RICHARD III. Why, Buckingham, I say, I would be king,
BUCKINGHAM. Why, so you are, my thrice renowned liege.
KING RICHARD III. Ha! am I king? 'tis so: but Edward lives.
BUCKINGHAM. True, noble prince.

---

[201] Shakespeare seems here to have spoken at random. The present scene is in 1483. Richard Duke of York, the husband of this lady, had he been then living, would have been but *seventy-three* years old, and we may reasonably suppose she was not older: nor did she go speedily to the grave; she lived till 1495.

[202] *Teen* seems to have been rather a favourite word with the Poet for *grief* or *sorrow*.

[203] To *play* the *touch* is to do the office of the *touchstone*, that is, a test, to prove the quality of a thing.

KING RICHARD III. O bitter consequence,
    That Edward still should live! *True, noble prince*!
    Cousin, thou wert not wont to be so dull:
    Shall I be plain? I wish the bastards dead;
    And I would have it suddenly perform'd.
    What sayest thou? speak suddenly,[204] be brief.
BUCKINGHAM. Your grace may do your pleasure.
KING RICHARD III. Tut, tut, thou art all ice, thy kindness freezeth:
    Say, have I thy consent that they shall die?
BUCKINGHAM. Give me some breath, some little pause, my lord
    Before I positively herein:
    I will resolve[205] your grace immediately. [*Exit.*]
CATESBY. [*Aside to another.*] The King is angry: see, he bites the lip.
KING RICHARD III. I will converse with iron-witted fools
    And unrespective boys:[206] [*Descends from his throne.*] none are for
        me
    That look into me with considerate eyes:
    High-reaching Buckingham grows circumspect.—
    Boy!—
PAGE. My lord?
KING RICHARD III. Know'st thou not any whom corrupting gold
    Would tempt unto a close exploit of death?
PAGE. My lord, I know a discontented gentleman,
    Whose humble means match not his haughty mind:
    Gold were as good as twenty orators,
    And will, no doubt, tempt him to any thing.
KING RICHARD III. What is his name?
PAGE. His name, my lord, is Tyrrel.
KING RICHARD III. I partly know the man: go, call him hither.—

[*Exit* Page.]

The deep-revolving witty[207] Buckingham
No more shall be the neighbour to my counsel:
Hath he so long held out with me untired,
And stops he now for breath?

[*Enter* STANLEY.]

---

[204] *Suddenly* is here the same as *quickly.*

[205] *Resolve* in the sense of *inform* or *satisfy*; a frequent usage.

[206] *Unrespective* is *inconsiderate* or *unthoughtful*; in accordance with the old use of *respect.* See page 87, note 191.

[207] *Witty* was employed to signify a *man of sagacity, wisdom,* or *judgment*; or, as Baret defines it, "*having the senses sharp, perceiving or foreseeing quicklie.*"

How now! what news with you?

STANLEY. My lord, I hear the Marquis Dorset's fled
 To Richmond, in those parts beyond the sea
 Where he abides.

KING RICHARD III. Come hither, Catesby: rumour it abroad
 That Anne, my wife, is sick and like to die:
 I will take order for her keeping close.
 Inquire me out some mean-born gentleman,
 Whom I will marry straight to Clarence' daughter:
 The boy is foolish,[208] and I fear not him.
 Look, how thou dream'st! I say again, give out
 That Anne my wife is sick and like to die:
 About it; for it stands me much upon,[209]
 To stop all hopes whose growth may damage me.—

[*Exit* CATESBY.]

I must be married to my brother's daughter,
Or else my kingdom stands on brittle glass.
Murder her brothers, and then marry her!
Uncertain way of gain! But I am in
So far in blood that sin will pluck on sin:
Tear-falling pity dwells not in this eye.—

[*Re-enter* Page, *with* TYRREL.]

Is thy name Tyrrel?

TYRREL. James Tyrrel, and your most obedient subject.

KING RICHARD III. Art thou, indeed?

TYRREL. Prove me, my gracious sovereign.

KING RICHARD III. Darest thou resolve to kill a friend of mine?

TYRREL. Ay, my lord;
 But I had rather kill two enemies.

KING RICHARD III. Why, there thou hast it: two deep enemies,
 Foes to my rest and my sweet sleep's disturbers
 Are they that I would have thee deal upon:
 Tyrrel, I mean those bastards in the Tower.

---

[208] This youth, who is known in history as Edward Earl of Warwick, was at that time but about ten years old. He was put to death by Henry VII. in 1499; he being then the only surviving male of the Plantagenet name. The chroniclers represent him as little better than an idiot; but his stupidity was most likely the result of cruel treatment; he being confined immediately after the battle of Bosworth, and his education totally neglected. It was the interest of the reigning powers to make him "foolish," or at least to have him thought so.

[209] This is an old idiomatic phrase for *it behoves me*, or, as we should now say, *it stands me in hand.*

TYRREL. Let me have open means to come to them,
    And soon I'll rid you from the fear of them.
KING RICHARD III. Thou sing'st sweet music. Hark, come hither,
    Tyrrel
    Go, by this token: rise, and lend thine ear: [*Whispers.*]
    There is no more but so: say it is done,
    And I will love thee, and prefer thee for it.
TYRREL. I will dispatch it straight. [*Exit.*]

    [*Re-enter* BUCKINGHAM.]

BUCKINGHAM. My Lord, I have consider'd in my mind
    The late demand that you did sound me in.
KING RICHARD III. Well, let that pass. Dorset is fled to Richmond.
BUCKINGHAM. I hear that news, my lord.
KING RICHARD III. Stanley, he is your wife's son well, look to it.
BUCKINGHAM. My lord, I claim your gift, my due by promise,
    For which your honour and your faith is pawn'd;
    The earldom of Hereford and the moveables
    The which you promised I should possess.
KING RICHARD III. Stanley, look to your wife; if she convey
    Letters to Richmond, you shall answer it.
BUCKINGHAM. What says your highness to my just demand?
KING RICHARD III. As I remember, Henry the Sixth
    Did prophesy that Richmond should be king,
    When Richmond was a little peevish boy.
    A king!—perhaps—
BUCKINGHAM. My lord,—
KING RICHARD III. How chance the prophet could not at that time
    Have told me, I being by, that I should kill him?
BUCKINGHAM. My lord, your promise for the earldom,—
KING RICHARD III. Richmond! When last I was at Exeter,
    The mayor in courtesy show'd me the castle,
    And call'd it Rougemont: at which name I started,
    Because a bard of Ireland told me once
    I should not live long after I saw Richmond.
BUCKINGHAM. My lord,—
KING RICHARD III. Ay, what's o'clock?
BUCKINGHAM. I am thus bold to put your grace in mind
    Of what you promised me.
KING RICHARD III. Well, but what's o'clock?
BUCKINGHAM. Upon the stroke of ten.
KING RICHARD III. Well, let it strike.
BUCKINGHAM. Why let it strike?

KING RICHARD III. Because that, like a Jack,[210] thou keep'st the stroke
    Betwixt thy begging and my meditation.
    I am not in the giving vein to-day.
BUCKINGHAM. Why, then resolve me whether you will or no.
KING RICHARD III. Tut, tut,
    Thou troublest me; am not in the vein.

    [*Exeunt all but* BUCKINGHAM.]

BUCKINGHAM. Is it even so? rewards he my true service
    With such deep contempt made I him king for this?
    O, let me think on Hastings, and be gone
    To Brecknock,[211] while my fearful head is on! [*Exit.*]

SCENE III.

Another Room in the Palace.

[*Enter* TYRREL.]

TYRREL. The tyrannous and bloody deed is done.
    The most arch of piteous massacre
    That ever yet this land was guilty of.
    Dighton and Forrest, whom I did suborn
    To do this ruthless piece of butchery,
    Although they were flesh'd[212] villains, bloody dogs,
    Melting with tenderness and kind compassion
    Wept like two children in their deaths' sad stories.
    O, thus, quoth Dighton, *lay those tender babes,—*
    Thus, thus, quoth Forrest, *girdling one another*
    Within their innocent alabaster arms:

---

[210] This alludes to the *Jack of the clock*, which was a figure made in old clocks to strike the hell on the outside. Richard compares Buckingham to one of the automatons, and bids him not to suspend the stroke on the clock bell, but strike, that the noise may be past, and himself at liberty to pursue his meditations. The following passage from Cotgrave will further elucidate its meaning: "A *jacke of the clocke-house*; a little busie-body, meddler, *jack-stickler*; one that has an care in every man's boat, or his hand in every man's dish."

[211] *Brecknock* was the name of Buckingham's castle in Wales.

[212] The verb to *flesh* is defined by Richardson "to train, to inure, to indulge, to glut or satiate." So in *Henry V.,* iii. 1: "And the *flesh'd* soldier, rough and hard of heart," &c. Also in Drayton's *Miseries of Queen Margaret:*

    Both which were *flesht* abundantly with blood
    In those three battles they had won before.

Their lips were four red roses on a stalk,
Which in their summer beauty kiss'd each other.
A book of prayers on their pillow lay;
Which once, quoth Forrest, *almost changed my mind;*
But O! the Devil—there the villain stopp'd
Whilst Dighton thus told on: *We smothered*
The most replenished sweet work of nature,
That from the prime creation e'er she framed.
Thus both are gone with conscience and remorse,[213]
They could not speak; and so I left them both,
To bring this tidings to the bloody king.
And here he comes.—

[*Enter King* RICHARD III.]

All hail, my sovereign liege!
KING RICHARD III. Kind Tyrrel, am I happy in thy news?
TYRREL. If to have done the thing you gave in charge
      Beget your happiness, be happy then,
      For it is done, my lord.
KING RICHARD III. But didst thou see them dead?
TYRREL. I did, my lord.
KING RICHARD III. And buried, gentle Tyrrel?
TYRREL. The chaplain of the Tower hath buried them;
      But how or in what place I do not know.
KING RICHARD III. Come to me, Tyrrel, soon at[214] after supper,
      And thou shalt tell the process of their death.
      Meantime, but think how I may do thee good,
      And be inheritor of thy desire.
      Farewell till soon.
TYRREL. I humbly take my leave. [*Exit.*]
KING RICHARD III. The son of Clarence have I pent up close;
      His daughter meanly have I match'd in marriage;[215]
      The sons of Edward sleep in Abraham's bosom,
      And Anne my wife hath bid the world good night.
      Now, for I know the Bretagne[216] Richmond aims
      At young Elizabeth, my brother's daughter,

---

[213] "Conscience and remorse" probably means what we call remorse of conscience, or, simply, remorse.

[214] Shakespeare has the phrase *soon* at several times in the sense of *about.*

[215] The daughter of Clarence was in fact married to Sir Richard Pole, and hence became the mother of Cardinal Pole. Sir Richard was half-brother to the Countess of Richmond.

[216] He thus denominates Richmond, because after the battle of Tewksbury he had taken refuge in the Court of Francis II., Duke of Bretagne, where by the procurement of Edward IV. he was kept a long time in honourable custody.

And, by that knot, looks proudly o'er the crown,
To her I go, a jolly thriving wooer.

[*Enter* CATESBY.]

CATESBY. My lord,—
KING RICHARD III. Good news or bad, that thou comest in so
   bluntly?
CATESBY. Bad news, my lord: Ely is fled to Richmond;
   And Buckingham, back'd with the hardy Welshmen,
   Is in the field, and still his power increaseth.
KING RICHARD III. Ely with Richmond troubles me more near
   Than Buckingham and his rash-levied army.
   Come, I have heard that fearful commenting
   Is leaden servitor to dull delay;[217]
   Delay leads impotent and snail-paced beggary
   Then fiery expedition be my wing,
   Jove's Mercury, and herald for a king![218]
   Come, muster men: my counsel is my shield;[219]
   We must be brief when traitors brave the field.[220] [*Exeunt.*]

SCENE IV.

The Same. Before the Palace.

[*Enter Queen* MARGARET.]

QUEEN MARGARET. So, now prosperity begins to mellow
   And drop into the rotten mouth of death.
   Here in these confines slyly have I lurk'd,
   To watch the waning of mine adversaries.
   A dire induction[221] am I witness to,

---

[217] *Fearful commenting* is timorous or cowardly reflection or deliberation; *leaden* of course is heavy or sluggish; *servitor* is an old form for *servant*; used whenever a trisyllable is wanted with that meaning; and *delay* is put for *procrastination* or reluctance to act. So that the sense is, cowardly deliberation is the tardy, lingering slave of a procrastinating spirit or master. The meaning of the next line is, that procrastination leads on to or superinduces feeble and creeping or slow-footed beggary.

[218] "Let my action be winged with the speed of lightning." Mercury was the old god of dispatch, and so was Jupiter's expressman. The text is made somewhat obscure by the omission of the relative; the sense being "expedition *who is* Jove's Mercury, and *so is* a king's *proper* herald."

[219] "My shield is my counsel, and shall deliberate the matter for me." He means that he is going to discuss or debate the issue not with words, but with knocks.

[220] To "brave the field" is, probably, to *challenge, dare,* or *defy* one *to* the field or to battle.—*Brief,* again, for *quick* or *speedy.*

[221] *Induction* here is *prologue* or *preparation.* See page 19, note 7.

And will to France, hoping the consequence
Will prove as bitter, black, and tragical.
Withdraw thee, wretched Margaret: who comes here? [*Retires.*]

[*Enter Queen* ELIZABETH *and the Duchess of* YORK.]

QUEEN ELIZABETH. Ah, my young princes! ah, my tender babes!
My unblown flowers, new-appearing sweets!
If yet your gentle souls fly in the air
And be not fix'd in doom perpetual,
Hover about me with your airy wings
And hear your mother's lamentation!
QUEEN MARGARET. [*Aside.*] Hover about her; say, that right for
right
Hath dimm'd your infant morn to aged night.[222]
DUCHESS OF YORK. So many miseries have crazed my voice,
That my woe-wearied tongue is mute and dumb,
Edward Plantagenet, why art thou dead?
QUEEN MARGARET. [*Aside.*] Plantagenet doth quit[223] Plantagenet.
Edward for Edward pays a dying debt.
QUEEN ELIZABETH. Wilt thou, O God, fly from such gentle lambs,
And throw them in the entrails of the wolf?
When didst thou sleep when such a deed was done?
QUEEN MARGARET. [*Aside.*] When holy Harry died, and my sweet
son.
DUCHESS OF YORK. Blind sight, dead life, poor mortal living ghost,
Woe's scene, world's shame, grave's due by life usurp'd,
Brief abstract and record of tedious days,
Rest thy unrest on England's lawful earth,[224] [*Sitting down.*]
Unlawfully made drunk with innocents' blood!
QUEEN ELIZABETH. O, that thou wouldst as well afford a grave
As thou canst yield a melancholy seat!
Then would I hide my bones, not rest them here.
O, who hath any cause to mourn but I?

---

[222] Meaning, apparently, that the Divine Justice, which was alleged in i. 3, as having righted others against her, and avenged the death of Rutland by that of her son Edward, is now turning upon her side, and righting her against others.

[223] To *quit* was often used for to *acquit*, and also for to *requite*. Here it may have either sense; perhaps it has both senses. Margaret may regard the death of her Edward as having been *avenged* by that of the other Edward; or she may think of the latter as offsetting, or atoning for' the former: so that the requital may itself serve for an acquittal.—To "pay a dying debt" is, I suppose, to pay a debt by dying.

[224] It is not very apparent why, or in what sense, *lawful* is here used: perhaps merely for a verbal antithesis to *unlawful*. Or is the speaker regarding England as the proper seat of order and law?

[*Sitting down by her.*]

QUEEN MARGARET. [*Coming forward.*] If ancient sorrow be most
    reverend,
  Give mine the benefit of seniory,[225]
  And let my woes frown on the upper hand.
  If sorrow can admit society,

[*Sitting down with them.*]

  Tell o'er your woes again by viewing mine:
  I had an Edward, till a Richard kill'd him;
  I had a Harry, till a Richard kill'd him:
  Thou hadst an Edward, till a Richard kill'd him;
  Thou hadst a Richard, till a Richard killed him;
DUCHESS OF YORK. I had a Richard too, and thou didst kill him;
  I had a Rutland too, thou holp'st to kill him.
QUEEN MARGARET. Thou hadst a Clarence too, and Richard kill'd
    him.
  From forth the kennel of thy womb hath crept
  A hell-hound that doth hunt us all to death:
  That dog, that had his teeth before his eyes,[226]
  To worry lambs and lap their gentle blood,
  That foul defacer of God's handiwork,
  That excellent grand tyrant of the earth,
  That reigns in galled eyes[227] of weeping souls,
  Thy womb let loose, to chase us to our graves.—
  O upright, just, and true-disposing God,
  How do I thank thee, that this carnal[228] cur
  Preys on the issue of his mother's body,
  And makes her pew-fellow[229] with others' moan!

---

[225] *Seniory* is but a shortened form of *seniority.*—*Ancient* here has the sense of *aged*
or *veteran.* Margaret's sorrow is *older* than that of the others.—To "frown on the upper
hand" is to have precedence in the right of expression.

[226] Alluding to the tradition that Richard, at his birth, had his mouth armed with
teeth. So, in v. 6, of *III Henry VI,* Richard says in reference to his birth,

> The midwife wonder'd, and the women cried,
> *O, Jesus bless us, he is born with teeth!*
> And so I was; which plainly signified
> That I should snarl, and bite, and play the dog.

[227] Eyes inflamed with weeping, or made red with "eye-offending brine." So in
Hamlet, i. 2: "The salt of most unrighteous tears had left the flushing in her galled eyes."
[228] *Carnal* for *sanguinary* or *blood-thirsty;* as in Hamlet, v. 2: "So shall you hear of
carnal, bloody, and unnatural acts."

DUCHESS OF YORK. O Harry's wife, triumph not in my woes!
    God witness with me, I have wept for thine.
QUEEN MARGARET. Bear with me; I am hungry for revenge,
    And now I cloy me with beholding it.
    Thy Edward he is dead, that stabb'd my Edward:
    Thy other Edward dead, to quit my Edward;
    Young York he is but boot,[230] because both they
    Match not the high perfection of my loss:
    Thy Clarence he is dead that kill'd my Edward;
    And the beholders of this tragic play,
    The adulterate[231] Hastings, Rivers, Vaughan, Grey,
    Untimely smother'd in their dusky graves.
    Richard yet lives, hell's black intelligencer,
    Only reserved their[232] factor, to buy souls
    And send them thither: but at hand, at hand,
    Ensues his piteous and unpitied end:
    Earth gapes, hell burns, fiends roar, saints pray.
    To have him suddenly convey'd away.
    Cancel his bond of life,[233] dear God, I prey,
    That I may live to say, *The dog is dead*!
QUEEN ELIZABETH. O, thou didst prophesy the time would come
    That I should wish for thee to help me curse
    That bottled spider, that foul bunch-back'd toad!
QUEEN MARGARET. I call'd thee then vain flourish of my fortune;
    I call'd thee then poor shadow, painted queen;
    The presentation of but what I was;
    The flattering index of a direful pageant;[234]
    One heaved a-high, to be hurl'd down below;
    A mother only mock'd with two sweet babes;
    A dream of what thou wert, a breath, a bubble,
    A sign of dignity, a garish flag,
    To be the aim of every dangerous shot;[235]
    A queen in jest, only to fill the scene.

---

[229] *Pew-fellow* is *companion* or *participator*. The Poet has *coach-fellow* in the same sense, apparently.

[230] *Boot* is an old word for any thing thrown into a bargain.

[231] *Adulterate* is *stained with adultery*. Alluding to Jane Shore.

[232] *Their* refers to *Hell*, which is used as a collective noun.—*Intelligencer* sometimes has the sense of *intelligencing* or *giving intelligence*. Here it seems to mean *spokesman, mouth-piece,* or *organ of communication*.—Of course *factor* is *agent*.

[233] The image is of a deed or indenture securing a life-tenure of property. So in *Macbeth*, iii. 2: "Cancel and tear to pieces that great bond which keeps me paled."

[234] The *index* of a pageant was probably a painted cloth hung up before a booth where a pageant was to be exhibited. See page 58, note 115.

[235] Alluding to the dangerous situation of those persons to whose care the standards of armies were intrusted.

Where is thy husband now? where be thy brothers?
Where are thy children? wherein dost thou, joy?
Who sues to thee and cries, *God save the queen*?
Where be the bending peers that flatter'd thee?
Where be the thronging troops that follow'd thee?
Decline all this,[236] and see what now thou art:
For happy wife, a most distressed widow;
For joyful mother, one that wails the name;
For queen, a very caitiff crown'd with care;
For one being sued to, one that humbly sues;
For one that scorn'd at me, now scorn'd of me;
For one being fear'd of all, now fearing one;
For one commanding all, obey'd of none.
Thus hath the course of justice wheel'd about,
And left thee but a very prey to time;
Having no more but thought of what thou wert,
To torture thee the more, being what thou art.
Thou didst usurp my place, and dost thou not
Usurp the just proportion of my sorrow?
Now thy proud neck bears half my burthen'd yoke;
From which even here I slip my weary neck,
And leave the burthen of it all on thee.
Farewell, York's wife, and queen of sad mischance:
These English woes will make me smile in France.
QUEEN ELIZABETH. O thou well skill'd in curses, stay awhile,
And teach me how to curse mine enemies!
QUEEN MARGARET. Forbear to sleep the nights, and fast the days;
Compare dead happiness with living woe;
Think that thy babes were fairer than they were,
And he that slew them fouler than he is:
Bettering[237] thy loss makes the bad causer worse:
Revolving this will teach thee how to curse.
QUEEN ELIZABETH. My words are dull; O, quicken them with thine!
QUEEN MARGARET. Thy woes will make them sharp, and pierce like
mine. [*Exit.*]
DUCHESS OF YORK. Why should calamity be full of words?
QUEEN ELIZABETH. Windy attorneys[238] to their client woes,

---

[236] That is, run it through all the moods and tenses.

[237] *Bettering* is here used in the sense of *exaggerating* or *magnifying*. "The greater
you conceive your loss to be, the worse the author of it will seem."

[238] Words are called "*windy* attorneys," because they are made up of wind. In his
Venus and Adonis the Poet figures the tongue as the heart's attorney:

> But when the heart's *attorney* once is mute,
> The *client* breaks, as desperate of his suit.

Airy succeeders of intestate joys,[239]
Poor breathing orators of miseries!
Let them have scope: though what they do impart
Help not all, yet do they ease the heart.[240]
DUCHESS OF YORK. If so, then be not tongue-tied: go with me.
And in the breath of bitter words let's smother
My damned son, which thy two sweet sons smother'd. [*Drum
within.*]
I hear his drum: be copious in exclaims.

[*Enter King* RICHARD III *and his Train, marching.*]

KING RICHARD III. Who intercepts my expedition?
DUCHESS OF YORK. O, she that might have intercepted thee,
By strangling thee in her accursed womb
From all the slaughters, wretch, that thou hast done!
QUEEN ELIZABETH. Hidest thou that forehead with a golden crown,
Where should be graven, if that right were right,
The slaughter of the prince that owed that crown,
And the dire death of my two sons and brothers?
Tell me, thou villain slave, where are my children?
DUCHESS OF YORK. Thou toad, thou toad, where is thy brother
Clarence?
And little Ned Plantagenet, his son?
QUEEN ELIZABETH. Where is kind Hastings, Rivers, Vaughan,
Grey?
KING RICHARD III. A flourish, trumpets! strike alarum, drums!
Let not the heavens hear these tell-tale women
Rail on the Lord's anointed: strike, I say!—

[*Flourish. Alarums.*]

Either be patient, and entreat me fair,
Or with the clamorous report of war
Thus will I drown your exclamations.
DUCHESS OF YORK. Art thou my son?
KING RICHARD III. Ay, I thank God, my father, and yourself.

---

[239] The joys, being all consumed and passed away, have died intestate; that is, have made no will, having nothing to bequeath; and mere verbal complaints are their successors, but inherit nothing but misery.

[240] This seems to have been rather a favourite idea with the Poet. So in *Macbeth*, iv. 3:

> Give sorrow words; the grief that does not speak
> Whispers the o'erfraught heart, and bids it break.

DUCHESS OF YORK. Then patiently hear my impatience.

KING RICHARD III. Madam, I have a touch of your condition,[241]
  Which cannot brook the accent of reproof.

DUCHESS OF YORK. O, let me speak!

KING RICHARD III. Do then: but I'll not hear.

DUCHESS OF YORK. I will be mild and gentle in my speech.

KING RICHARD III. And brief, good mother; for I am in haste.

DUCHESS OF YORK. Art thou so hasty? I have stay'd for thee,
  God knows, in anguish, pain and agony.

KING RICHARD III. And came I not at last to comfort you?

DUCHESS OF YORK. No, by the holy rood, thou know'st it well,
  Thou camest on earth to make the earth my hell.
  A grievous burthen was thy birth to me;
  Tetchy and wayward was thy infancy;
  Thy school-days frightful, desperate, wild, and furious,
  Thy prime of manhood daring, bold, and venturous,
  Thy age confirm'd, proud, subdued, bloody, treacherous,
  More mild, but yet more harmful, kind in hatred:
  What comfortable hour canst thou name,
  That ever graced me in thy company?

KING RICHARD III. Faith, none, but Humphrey Hower,[242] that call'd
    your grace
  To breakfast once forth of my company.
  If I be so disgracious in your eye,
  Let me march on, and not offend you, madam.—
  Strike the drum.

DUCHESS OF YORK. I prithee, hear me speak.

KING RICHARD III. You speak too bitterly.

DUCHESS OF YORK. Hear me a word;
  For I shall never speak to thee again.

KING RICHARD III. So.

---

[241] A *smack* or *spice* of your *disposition* or *temper*.

[242] So printed in the old copies. No satisfactory explanation of the passage has yet been discovered. A part of St. Paul's Cathedral was called Duke Humphrey's Walk, because Humphrey, sometime Duke of Gloucester, was supposed to be buried there. As the old Cathedral was a place of great resort, those who were hard up for a dinner used to saunter there, perhaps in the hope of being asked to dinner by some of their acquaintance. Hence grew the phrase of "dining with Duke Humphrey," used of those who thus "waited upon Providence" for a chance to eat. And Steevens thinks that "Shakespeare might by this strange phrase, *Humphrey Hour*, have designed to mark the hour at which the good Duchess was as hungry as the followers of Duke Humphrey." Singer thinks "it is possible that by *Humphrey Hower* Richard alludes to the hour of his birth, the *hour* after which his mother ate out of his company." And he quotes the old vulgar saying, that a teeming woman feeds two. According to this, *Humphrey Hower* might he meant as the name of the physician who attended the Duchess when her Richard was born. Staunton "apprehends that *Humphrey Hour* was nothing more than a cant phrase for *eating-hour*." None of these explanations can hold my assent, nor can I think of any better.

DUCHESS OF YORK. Either thou wilt die, by God's just ordinance,
  Ere from this war thou turn a conqueror,
  Or I with grief and extreme age shall perish
  And never look upon thy face again.
  Therefore take with thee my most heavy curse;
  Which, in the day of battle, tire thee more
  Than all the complete armour that thou wear'st!
  My prayers on the adverse party fight;
  And there the little souls of Edward's children
  Whisper the spirits of thine enemies
  And promise them success and victory.
  Bloody thou art, bloody will be thy end;
  Shame serves thy life and doth thy death attend. [*Exit.*]
QUEEN ELIZABETH. Though far more cause, yet much less spirit to
    curse
  Abides in me; I say amen to her. [*Going.*]
KING RICHARD III. Stay, madam; I must speak a word with you.
QUEEN ELIZABETH. I have no more sons of the royal blood
  For thee to murder: for my daughters, Richard,
  They shall be praying nuns, not weeping queens;
  And therefore level not to hit their lives.
KING RICHARD III. You have a daughter call'd Elizabeth,
  Virtuous and fair, royal and gracious.
QUEEN ELIZABETH. And must she die for this? O, let her live,
  And I'll corrupt her manners, stain her beauty;
  Slander myself as false to Edward's bed;
  Throw over her the veil of infamy:
  So she may live unscarr'd of bleeding slaughter,
  I will confess she was not Edward's daughter.
KING RICHARD III. Wrong not her birth, she is of royal blood.
QUEEN ELIZABETH. To save her life, I'll say she is not so.
KING RICHARD III. Her life is only safest in her birth.
QUEEN ELIZABETH. And only in that safety died her brothers.
KING RICHARD III. Lo, at their births good stars were opposite.
QUEEN ELIZABETH. No, to their lives bad friends were contrary.
KING RICHARD III. All unavoided[243] is the doom of destiny.
QUEEN ELIZABETH. True, when avoided grace makes destiny:
  My babes were destined to a fairer death,
  If grace had bless'd thee with a fairer life.
KING RICHARD III. You speak as if that I had slain my cousins.
QUEEN ELIZABETH. Cousins, indeed; and by their uncle cozen'd
  Of comfort, kingdom, kindred, freedom, life.

---

[243] *Unavoided* for *unavoidable.* So the endings *-ed* and *-able* were often used indiscriminately.

Whose hand soever lanced their tender hearts,
Thy head, all indirectly,[244] gave direction:
No doubt the murderous knife was dull and blunt
Till it was whetted on thy stone-hard heart,
To revel in the entrails of my lambs.
But that still[245] use of grief makes wild grief tame,
My tongue should to thy ears not name my boys
Till that my nails were anchor'd in thine eyes;
And I, in such a desperate bay of death,
Like a poor bark, of sails and tackling reft,
Rush all to pieces on thy rocky bosom.

KING RICHARD III. Madam, so thrive I in my enterprise
And dangerous success of bloody wars,[246]
As I intend more good to you and yours,
Than ever you or yours were by me wrong'd!

QUEEN ELIZABETH. What good is cover'd with the face of heaven,
To be discover'd, that can do me good?

KING RICHARD III. The advancement of your children, gentle lady.

QUEEN ELIZABETH. Up to some scaffold, there to lose their heads?

KING RICHARD III. No, to the dignity and height of honour
The high imperial type of this Earth's glory.[247]

QUEEN ELIZABETH. Flatter my sorrows with report of it;
Tell me what state, what dignity, what honour,
Canst thou demise[248] to any child of mine?

KING RICHARD III. Even all I have; yea, and myself and all,
Will I withal endow a child of thine;
So in the Lethe of thy angry soul
Thou drown the sad remembrance of those wrongs
Which thou supposest I have done to thee.

QUEEN ELIZABETH. Be brief, lest that be process of thy kindness
Last longer telling than thy kindness' date.

KING RICHARD III. Then know, that from my soul I love thy daughter.

QUEEN ELIZABETH. My daughter's mother thinks it with her soul.

KING RICHARD III. What do you think?

QUEEN ELIZABETH. That thou dost love my daughter from thy soul:
So from thy soul's love didst thou love her brothers;

---

[244] *Indirectly* here means *wrongfully* or *wickedly*; probably used for a sort of jingle with *direction*. It may be worth noting, however, that the radical sense of *right*, as also of *direct*, is *straight*; while that of *wrong*, as also of *indirect*, is *crooked*.

[245] The use of *still* for *continually* is very frequent: here it is used as an adjective with the same sense, *continual*.

[246] That is, the bloody wars that are to *follow*; *success* being used in the Latin sense of *succession* or *sequel*.

[247] That is, the *crown*, the emblem of royalty.

[248] To *demise* is to *grant*, from *demittere*, Latin.

And from my heart's love,[249] I do thank thee for it.

KING RICHARD III. Be not so hasty to confound my meaning:
I mean, that with my soul I love thy daughter,
And mean to make her queen of England.

QUEEN ELIZABETH. Say then, who dost thou mean shall be her king?

KING RICHARD III. Even he that makes her queen who should be else?

QUEEN ELIZABETH. What, thou?

KING RICHARD III. I, even I: what think you of it, madam?

QUEEN ELIZABETH. How canst thou woo her?

KING RICHARD III. That would I learn of you,
As one that are best acquainted with her humour.

QUEEN ELIZABETH. And wilt thou learn of me?

KING RICHARD III. Madam, with all my heart.

QUEEN ELIZABETH. Send to her, by the man that slew her brothers,
A pair of bleeding-hearts; thereon engrave
Edward and York; then haply she will weep:
Therefore present to her—as sometime Margaret
Did to thy father, steep'd in Rutland's blood,—
A handkerchief; which, say to her, did drain
The purple sap from her sweet brother's body
And bid her dry her weeping eyes therewith.
If this inducement force her not to love,
Send her a story of thy noble acts;
Tell her thou madest away her uncle Clarence,
Her uncle Rivers; yea, and, for her sake,
Madest quick conveyance with her good aunt Anne.

KING RICHARD III. Come, come, you mock me; this is not the way
To win our daughter.

QUEEN ELIZABETH. There is no other way
Unless thou couldst put on some other shape,
And not be Richard that hath done all this.

KING RICHARD III. Say that I did all this for love of her.

QUEEN ELIZABETH. Nay, then indeed she cannot choose but hate thee,
Having bought love with such a bloody spoil.

KING RICHARD III. Look, what is done cannot be now amended:
Men shall[250] deal unadvisedly sometimes,
Which after hours give leisure to repent.

---

[249] The Queen is quibbling between the different senses of *from*; one of which is *out of*, as when we say, "Speak the truth *from* the heart"; the other, that of separation or distance, as when Hamlet says "any thing so overdone is *from the purpose* of playing."

[250] *Shall* for *will*; the two being often used indiscriminately.—*Unadvisedly* in the old sense of *inconsiderately, rashly,* or *imprudently*. See page 40, note 74.

If I did take the kingdom from your sons,
To make amends, Ill give it to your daughter.
If I have kill'd the issue of your womb,
To quicken your increase, I will beget
Mine issue of your blood upon your daughter
A grandam's name is little less in love
Than is the doting title of a mother;
They are as children but one step below,
Even of your mettle, of your very blood;
Of an one pain,—save for a night of groans
Endured of her, for whom you bid[251] like sorrow.
Your children were vexation to your youth,
But mine shall be a comfort to your age.
The loss you have is but a son being king,
And by that loss your daughter is made queen.
I cannot make you what amends I would,
Therefore accept such kindness as I can.
Dorset your son, that with a fearful soul
Leads discontented steps in foreign soil,
This fair alliance quickly shall call home
To high promotions and great dignity:
The king, that calls your beauteous daughter wife.
Familiarly shall call thy Dorset brother;
Again shall you be mother to a king,
And all the ruins of distressful times
Repair'd with double riches of content.
What! we have many goodly days to see:
The liquid drops of tears that you have shed
Shall come again, transform'd to orient pearl,
Advantaging their loan with interest
Of ten times double gain of happiness.
Go, then my mother, to thy daughter go
Make bold her bashful years with your experience;
Prepare her ears to hear a wooer's tale
Put in her tender heart the aspiring flame
Of golden sovereignty; acquaint the princess
With the sweet silent hours of marriage joys
And when this arm of mine hath chastised
The petty rebel, dull-brain'd Buckingham,
Bound with triumphant garlands will I come
And lead thy daughter to a conqueror's bed;

---

[251] "Endured *of* her" is the same as endured *by* her; of being formerly used in such cases to denote the relation of agent.—*Bid* is an old preterite form for *bided, suffered,* or *endured.*

To whom I will retail[252] my conquest won,

And she shall be sole victress, Caesar's Caesar.

QUEEN ELIZABETH. What were I best to say? her father's brother

Would be her lord? or shall I say, her uncle?

Or, he that slew her brothers and her uncles?

Under what title shall I woo for thee,

That God, the law, my honour and her love,

Can make seem pleasing to her tender years?

KING RICHARD III. Infer fair England's peace by this alliance.

QUEEN ELIZABETH. Which she shall purchase with still lasting war.

KING RICHARD III. Say that the king, which may command, entreats.

QUEEN ELIZABETH. That at her hands which the king's King forbids.

KING RICHARD III. Say, she shall be a high and mighty queen.

QUEEN ELIZABETH. To wail the tide, as her mother doth.

KING RICHARD III. Say, I will love her everlastingly.

QUEEN ELIZABETH. But how long shall that title[253] *ever* last?

KING RICHARD III. Sweetly in force unto her fair life's end.

QUEEN ELIZABETH. But how long fairly shall her sweet lie last?

KING RICHARD III. So long as heaven and nature lengthens it.

QUEEN ELIZABETH. So long as hell and Richard likes of it.

KING RICHARD III. Say, I, her sovereign, am her subject love.

QUEEN ELIZABETH. But she, your subject, loathes such sovereignty.

KING RICHARD III. Be eloquent in my behalf to her.

QUEEN ELIZABETH. An honest tale speeds best being plainly told.

KING RICHARD III. Then in plain terms tell her my loving tale.

QUEEN ELIZABETH. Plain and not honest is too harsh a style.

KING RICHARD III. Your reasons are too shallow and too quick.

QUEEN ELIZABETH. O no, my reasons are too deep and dead;[254]

Too deep and dead, poor infants, in their grave.

KING RICHARD III. Harp not on that string, madam; that is past.

QUEEN ELIZABETH. Harp on it still shall I till heart-strings break.

KING RICHARD III. Now, by my George,[255] my garter, and my crown,—

QUEEN ELIZABETH. Profaned, dishonour'd, and the third usurp'd.

KING RICHARD III.—I swear—

QUEEN ELIZABETH. By nothing; for this is no oath:

The George, profaned, hath lost his holy honour;

---

[252] *Retail*, again, for *recount* or *tell over*. See page 65, note 128.

[253] The word *title* is here used in a legal or forensic sense, for interest in an estate. So says Heath.

[254] The Queen implies an equivoque on *quick*, which is used by Richard in the sense of *prompt, nimble, or rash*; and she plays between this sense and that of *alive*.

[255] This was a figure or image of St. George on horseback, which was worn as a badge by Knights of the Garter.

The garter, blemish'd, pawn'd his knightly virtue;
The crown, usurp'd, disgraced his kingly glory.
If something thou wilt swear to be believed,
Swear then by something that thou hast not wrong'd.
KING RICHARD III. Now, by the world,—
QUEEN ELIZABETH. 'Tis full of thy foul wrongs.
KING RICHARD III. My father's death,—
QUEEN ELIZABETH. Thy life hath that dishonour'd.
KING RICHARD III. Then, by myself,—
QUEEN ELIZABETH. Thyself thyself misusest.
KING RICHARD III. Why then, by God,—
QUEEN ELIZABETH. God's wrong is most of all.
    If thou hadst fear'd to break an oath by Him,
    The unity the king thy brother made
    Had not been broken, nor my brother slain:
    If thou hadst fear'd to break an oath by Him,
    The imperial metal, circling now thy brow,
    Had graced the tender temples of my child,
    And both the princes had been breathing here,
    Which now, two tender playfellows to dust,
    Thy broken faith hath made a prey for worms.
    What canst thou swear by now?
KING RICHARD III. The time to come.
QUEEN ELIZABETH. That thou hast wronged in the time o'erpast;
    For I myself have many tears to wash
    Hereafter time, for time past wrong'd by thee.
    The children live, whose parents thou hast slaughter'd,
    Ungovern'd youth, to wail it in their age;
    The parents live, whose children thou hast butcher'd,
    Old wither'd plants, to wail it with their age.
    Swear not by time to come; for that thou hast
    Misused ere used, by time misused o'erpast.
KING RICHARD III. As I intend to prosper and repent,
    So thrive I in my dangerous attempt
    Of hostile arms! myself myself confound!
    Heaven and fortune bar me happy hours!
    Day, yield me not thy light; nor, night, thy rest!
    Be opposite all planets of good luck
    To my proceedings!—if, with pure heart's love,
    Immaculate devotion, holy thoughts,
    I tender not thy beauteous princely daughter!
    In her consists my happiness and thine;
    Without her, follows to this land and me,
    To thee, herself, and many a Christian soul,
    Death, desolation, ruin and decay:

It cannot be avoided but by this;
It will not be avoided but by this.
Therefore, good mother,—I must can you so,—
Be the attorney of my love to her:
Plead what I will be, not what I have been;
Not my deserts, but what I will deserve:
Urge the necessity and state of times,
And be not peevish-fond[256] in great designs.
QUEEN ELIZABETH. Shall I be tempted of the devil thus?
KING RICHARD III. Ay, if the devil tempt thee to do good.
QUEEN ELIZABETH. Shall I forget myself to be myself?
KING RICHARD III. Ay, if yourself's remembrance wrong yourself.
QUEEN ELIZABETH. But thou didst kill my children.
KING RICHARD III. But in your daughter's womb I bury them:
Where in that nest of spicery they shall breed
Selves of themselves, to your recomforture.
QUEEN ELIZABETH. Shall I go win my daughter to thy will?
KING RICHARD III. And be a happy mother by the deed.
QUEEN ELIZABETH. I go.—Write to me very shortly.
And you shall understand from me her mind.[257]
KING RICHARD III. Bear her my true love's kiss; and so, farewell.—

[*Kissing her. Exit Queen* ELIZABETH.]

Relenting fool, and shallow, changing woman!—

[*Enter* RATCLIFF; CATESBY *following.*]

How now! what news?
RATCLIFF. My gracious sovereign, on the western coast
Rideth a puissant navy; to the shore
Throng many doubtful hollow-hearted friends,
Unarm'd, and unresolved to beat them back:
'Tis thought that Richmond is their admiral;
And there they hull,[258] expecting but the aid
Of Buckingham to welcome them ashore.

---

[256] Both *fond* and *peevish* are often used by Shakespeare for *foolish*. So in scene 2 of this Act: "When Richmond was a little *peevish* boy." The compound seems to have about the same meaning as *childish-foolish*, which occurs in i. 3, of this play. Or *peevish* may here have the sense of *perverse*.

[257] This representation is in substance historical; and some of the old chroniclers are rather hard on Elizabeth for thus yielding to Richard's persuasions. But there is good reason to think that she outwitted him, and that her consent was but feigned in order to gain time, and to save her daughter from the fate that had overtaken her sons.

[258] A ship is said to *hull* when she hauls in her sails, and lays-to, without coming to anchor, and so floats hither and thither as the waves carry her.

KING RICHARD III. Some light-foot friend post to the Duke of
    Norfolk:—
    Ratcliff, thyself,—or Catesby; where is he?
CATESBY. Here, my lord.
KING RICHARD III. Fly to the duke.—[*To* RATCLIFF.] Post thou to
    Salisbury
    When thou comest thither,—[*To* CATESBY.] Dull, unmindful
    villain,
    Why stand'st thou still, and go'st not to the duke?
CATESBY. First, mighty sovereign, let me know your mind,
    What from your grace I shall deliver to him.
KING RICHARD III. O, true, good Catesby: bid him levy straight
    The greatest strength and power he can make,
    And meet me presently at Salisbury.
CATESBY. I go. [*Exit.*]
RATCLIFF. What is't your highness' pleasure I shall do at Salisbury?
KING RICHARD III. Why, what wouldst thou do there before I go?
RATCLIFF. Your highness told me I should post before.

[*Enter* STANLEY.]

KING RICHARD III. My mind is changed.—Stanley, what news with
    you?
STANLEY. None good, my lord, to please you with the hearing;
    Nor none so bad, but it may well be told.
KING RICHARD III. Hoyday, a riddle! neither good nor bad!
    Why dost thou run so many mile about,
    When thou mayst tell thy tale a nearer way?
    Once more, what news?
STANLEY. Richmond is on the seas.
KING RICHARD III. There let him sink, and be the seas on him!
    White-liver'd runagate,[259] what doth he there?
STANLEY. I know not, mighty sovereign, but by guess.
KING RICHARD III. Well, sir, as you guess, as you guess?
STANLEY. Stirr'd up by Dorset, Buckingham, and Ely,
    He makes for England, there to claim the crown.
KING RICHARD III. Is the chair empty? is the sword unsway'd?
    Is the king dead? the empire unpossess'd?
    What heir of York is there alive but we?
    And who is England's king but great York's heir?
    Then, tell me, what doth he upon the sea?

---

[259] *Runagate* is *runaway* or *vagabond*. *White-liver'd, lily-liver'd,* and *milk-livered*
are terms denoting extreme cowardice. In v. 3, Richard calls Richmond "a milksop."
Richmond had in fact escaped the fate of the Lancastrian leaders by fleeing into France.

STANLEY. Unless for that, my liege, I cannot guess.

KING RICHARD III. Unless for that²⁶⁰ he comes to be your liege,
  You cannot guess wherefore the Welshman comes.
  Thou wilt revolt, and fly to him, I fear.

STANLEY. No, mighty liege; therefore mistrust me not.

KING RICHARD III. Where is thy power, then, to beat him back?
  Where are thy tenants and thy followers?
  Are they not now upon the western shore.
  Safe-conducting the rebels from their ships!

STANLEY. No, my good lord, my friends are in the north.

KING RICHARD III. Cold friends to Richard: what do they in the
      north,
  When they should serve their sovereign in the west?

STANLEY. They have not been commanded, mighty sovereign:
  Please it your majesty to give me leave,
  I'll muster up my friends, and meet your grace
  Where and what time your majesty shall please.

KING RICHARD III. Ay, ay. thou wouldst be gone to join with
Richmond:
  I will not trust you, sir.

STANLEY. Most mighty sovereign,
  You have no cause to hold my friendship doubtful:
  I never was nor never will be false.

KING RICHARD III. Well,
  Go muster men; but, hear you, leave behind
  Your son, George Stanley: look your faith be firm.
  Or else his head's assurance is but frail.

STANLEY. So deal with him as I prove true to you. [*Exit.*]

[*Enter a* MESSENGER.]

MESSENGER. My gracious sovereign, now in Devonshire,
  As I by friends am well advertised,²⁶¹
  Sir Edward Courtney, and the haughty prelate
  Bishop of Exeter, his brother there,
  With many more confederates, are in arms.

[*Enter a second* MESSENGER.]

SECOND MESSENGER. My liege, in Kent the Guildfords are in arms;
  And every hour more competitors²⁶²

---

²⁶⁰ The words *for that* are here equivalent to *because*; a common usage with the old writers. Richard chooses to take the phrase in another sense than Stanley had meant.

²⁶¹ *Advertised* for *informed, notified,* or *instructed,* occurs repeatedly.

²⁶² *Competitors* for *confederates* or *partners.*

Flock to their aid, and still their power increaseth.

[*Enter a third* MESSENGER.]

THIRD MESSENGER. My lord, the army of the Duke of
    Buckingham—
KING RICHARD III. Out on you, owls! nothing but songs of death?[263]

[*Strikes him.*]

Take that, until thou bring me better news.
THIRD MESSENGER. The news I have to tell your majesty
    Is, that by sudden floods and fall of waters,
    Buckingham's army is dispersed and scatter'd;
    And he himself wander'd away alone,
    No man knows whither.
KING RICHARD III. I cry thee mercy:
    There is my purse to cure that blow of thine.
    Hath any well-advised friend proclaim'd
    Reward to him that brings the traitor in?
THIRD MESSENGER. Such proclamation hath been made, my liege.

[*Enter a fourth* MESSENGER.]

FOURTH MESSENGER. Sir Thomas Lovel and Lord Marquis Dorset,
    'Tis said, my liege, in Yorkshire are in arms.
    Yet this good comfort bring I to your grace,
    The Breton navy is dispersed by tempest:
    Richmond, in Yorkshire, sent out a boat
    Unto the shore, to ask those on the banks
    If they were his assistants, yea or no;
    Who answer'd him, they came from Buckingham.
    Upon his party:[264] he, mistrusting them,
    Hoisted sail and made away for Brittany.
KING RICHARD III. March on, march on, since we are up in arms;
    If not to fight with foreign enemies,
    Yet to beat down these rebels here at home.

[*Re-enter* CATESBY.]

CATESBY. My liege, the Duke of Buckingham is taken;
    That is the best news: that the Earl of Richmond

---

[263] The owl's note or hoot was considered ominous or ill-boding.
[264] "Upon his party" is to take part with him; to fight on his side.

Is with a mighty power landed at Milford,
Is colder tidings, yet they must be told.[265]
KING RICHARD III. Away towards Salisbury! while we reason
    here,[266]
A royal battle might be won and lost:—
Some one take order[267] Buckingham be brought
To Salisbury; the rest march on with me. [*Flourish. Exeunt.*]

SCENE V.

A Room in Lord STANLEY'*s House.*

[*Enter* STANLEY *and* SIR CHRISTOPHER URSWICK.]

STANLEY. Sir Christopher, tell Richmond this from me:
    That in the sty of this most bloody boar
    My son George Stanley is frank'd up in hold:
    If I revolt, off goes young George's head;
    The fear of that withholds my present aid.
    But, tell me, where is princely Richmond now?
CHRISTOPHER. At Pembroke, or at Ha'rford-west,[268] in Wales.
STANLEY. What men of name resort to him?
CHRISTOPHER. Sir Walter Herbert, a renowned soldier;
    Sir Gilbert Talbot, Sir William Stanley;
    Oxford, redoubted Pembroke, Sir James Blunt,
    And Rhys ap Thomas with a valiant crew;
    And many more of noble fame and worth:
    And towards London they do bend[269] their course,
    If by the way they be not fought withal.
STANLEY. Return unto thy lord; commend me to him:
    Tell him the queen hath heartily consented
    He shall espouse Elizabeth her daughter.
    These letters will resolve[270] him of my mind. [*Giving letters.*]
    Farewell. [*Exeunt.*]

---

[265] The Earl of Richmond embarked with about two thousand men at Harfleur, in Normandy, August 1, 1485, and landed at Milford Haven on the 7th. He directed his course to Wales, hoping the Welsh would receive him cordially as their countryman, he having been born at Pembroke, and his grandfather being Owen Tudor, who married Catharine of France, the widow of Henry the Fifth and mother of Henry the Sixth.

[266] That is, "while we *are talking* here." See page 60, note 119.

[267] To *take order* is, in old English, to adopt measures, or give directions.

[268] This name in full is *Haverford*-West; shortened for metre's sake, of course. The place lies nearly north of Pembroke.

[269] To *bend* occurs often in the sense of to *direct*.

[270] *Resolve*, again, for *inform* or *satisfy*. See page 94, note 205.

ACT V.

SCENE I.

Salisbury. An open Place.

[*Enter the* SHERIFF, *and Guard, with* BUCKINGHAM, *led to Execution.*]

BUCKINGHAM. Will not King Richard let me speak with him?
SHERIFF. No, my good lord; therefore be patient.
BUCKINGHAM. Hastings, and Edward's children, Rivers, Grey,
    Holy King Henry, and thy fair son Edward,
    Vaughan, and all that have miscarried
    By underhand corrupted foul injustice,—
    If that your moody discontented souls
    Do through the clouds behold this present hour,
    Even for revenge mock my destruction!—
    This is All-Souls' day, fellows, is it not?
SHERIFF. It is, my lord.
BUCKINGHAM. Why, then All-Souls' day[271] is my body's doomsday.
    This is the day that, in King Edward's time,
    I wish't might fall on me, when I was found
    False to his children or his wife's allies
    This is the day wherein I wish'd to fall
    By the false faith of him I trusted most;
    This, this All-Souls' day to my fearful soul
    Is the determined respite of my wrongs:[272]
    That high All-Seer that I dallied with
    Hath turn'd my feigned prayer on my head
    And given in earnest what I begg'd in jest.
    Thus doth he force the swords of wicked men
    To turn their own points on their masters' bosoms:
    Now Margaret's curse is fallen upon my head;
    When he, quoth she, *shall split thy heart with sorrow,*
    Remember Margaret was a prophetess.—
    Come, sirs, convey me to the block of shame;
    Wrong hath but wrong, and blame the due of blame. [*Exeunt.*]

---

[271] Buckingham was executed on All-Saints' day, November 1, 1483.
[272] That is, "the *close* or *termination* of the period for which the punishment of my crimes was *deferred.*

SCENE II.

Plain near Tamworth.

[*Enter, with drum and colours,* RICHMOND,[273] OXFORD,[274] *Sir* JAMES BLUNT, *Sir* WALTER HERBERT, *and others, with Forces, marching.*]

RICHMOND. Fellows in arms, and my most loving friends,
    Bruised underneath the yoke of tyranny,
    Thus far into the bowels of the land
    Have we march'd on without impediment;
    And here receive we from our father Stanley
    Lines of fair comfort and encouragement.
    The wretched, bloody, and usurping boar,
    That spoil'd your summer fields and fruitful vines,
    Swills your warm blood like wash, and makes his trough
    In your embowell'd bosoms,—this foul swine
    Lies now even in the centre of this isle,
    Near to the town of Leicester, as we learn
    From Tamworth thither is but one day's march.
    In God's name, cheerly on, courageous friends,
    To reap the harvest of perpetual peace
    By this one bloody trial of sharp war.
OXFORD. Every man's conscience is a thousand swords,
    To fight against that bloody homicide.
HERBERT. I doubt not but his friends will fly to us.
BLUNT. He hath no friends but who are friends for fear.
    Which in his greatest need will shrink from him.
RICHMOND. All for our vantage. Then, in God's name, march:
    True hope is swift, and flies with swallow's wings:
    Kings it makes gods, and meaner creatures kings. [*Exeunt.*]

---

[273] It has already been noted that on his father's side the Earl of Richmond was grandson to Owen Tudor. His mother was Margaret, daughter and heir to John Beaufort, the first Duke of Somerset, and great-granddaughter to John of Ghent by Catharine Swynford; on which account, after the death of Henry VI. and his son, Richmond was looked to by both friends and foes as the next male representative of the Lancastrian line. The Lancastrians all regarded him as their natural chief; and many of the Yorkists accepted him because of his having bound himself by solemn oath to marry the Princess Elizabeth, whom they of course considered the rightful heir to the crown after the death of her brothers.

[274] This Earl of Oxford was John de Vere, whose character, together with that of his son Arthur, is so finely delineated in Scott's *Anne of Geierstein.*

SCENE III.

Bosworth Field.

[*Enter King* RICHARD III *and Forces, the Duke of* NORFOLK, *Earl of* SURREY, *and others.*]

KING RICHARD III. Here pitch our tents, even here in Bosworth
    field.—
    My Lord of Surrey, why look you so sad?
SURREY. My heart is ten times lighter than my looks.
KING RICHARD III. My Lord of Norfolk,—
NORFOLK. Here, most gracious liege.
KING RICHARD III. Norfolk, we must have knocks; ha! must we not?
NORFOLK. We must both give and take, my gracious lord.
KING RICHARD III. Up with my tent there! here will I lie tonight;

[*Soldiers begin to set up his tent.*]

    But where to-morrow? Well, all's one for that.—
    Who hath descried the number of the foe?
NORFOLK. Six or seven thousand is their utmost power.
KING RICHARD III. Why, our battalion trebles that account:[275]
    Besides, the king's name is a tower of strength,
    Which they upon the adverse party want.
    Up with my tent there! Valiant gentlemen,
    Let us survey the vantage of the field
    Call for some men of sound direction:[276]
    Let's want no discipline, make no delay,
    For, lords, to-morrow is a busy day. [*Exeunt.*]

[*Enter, on the other side of the field,* RICHMOND, *Sir* WILLIAM
    BRANDON, OXFORD, *and others. Some of the* Soldiers
    pitch RICHMOND's *tent.*]

RICHMOND. The weary sun hath made a golden set,
    And by the bright track of his fiery car,
    Gives signal, of a goodly day to-morrow.—
    Sir William Brandon, you shall bear my standard.—

---

[275] Richmond's forces are said to have been only five thousand; and Richard's army consisted of about twelve thousand. But Lord Stanley lay at a small distance with three thousand men, and Richard may be supposed to have reckoned on them as his friends, though the event proved otherwise.

[276] Men of tried judgment and approved military skill.

Give me some ink and paper in my tent
I'll draw the form and model of our battle,
Limit[277] each leader to his several charge,
And part in just proportion our small power.—
My Lord of Oxford,—you, Sir William Brandon,—
And you, Sir Walter Herbert,—stay with me.—
The Earl of Pembroke keeps his regiment:[278]—
Good Captain Blunt, bear my good night to him
And by the second hour in the morning
Desire the earl to see me in my tent:
Yet one thing more, good captain, do for me,—
Where is Lord Stanley quarter'd,[279] dost thou know?
BLUNT. Unless I have mista'en his colours much,—
Which well I am assured I have not done,—
His regiment lies half a mile at least
South from the mighty power of the king.
RICHMOND. If without peril it be possible,
Good Captain Blunt, bear my good-night to him,
And give him from me this most needful scroll.
BLUNT. Upon my life, my lord, I'll under-take it;
And so, God give you quiet rest to-night!
RICHMOND. Good night, good Captain Blunt. [*Exit* BLUNT.]
        —Come gentlemen,
Let us consult upon to-morrow's business
In to our tent; the air is raw and cold.

[*They withdraw into the tent.*]

[*Re-enter, to his tent, King* RICHARD III, NORFOLK,
RATCLIFF, CATESBY, *and others.*]

KING RICHARD III. What is't o'clock?
CATESBY. It's supper-time, my lord;
        It's nine o'clock.
KING RICHARD III. I will not sup to-night.—
        What, is my beaver easier than it was?[280]

---

[277] That is, *direct* or *appoint* the leaders what part they are *separately* to perform in the forthcoming conflict. The Poet has to *limit* repeatedly so. See page 73, note 148.

[278] "*Keeps* his *regiment*" is, in our phrase, *remains with* his *command*; *regiment* being used, not for the regimental portion of an army, but in the old sense of *government*. So, in the next speech, it is said that Lord Stanley's "regiment lies half a mile at least south from the mighty power of the King.—*Keep* is repeatedly used by the Poet for *dwell* or *stay*.

[279] To *quarter* is still in use as a military term for to *lodge* or *encamp*.

And all my armour laid into my tent?

CATESBY. If is, my liege; and all things are in readiness.

KING RICHARD III. Good Norfolk, hie thee to thy charge;
    Use careful watch, choose trusty sentinels.

NORFOLK. I go, my lord.

KING RICHARD III. Stir with the lark to-morrow, gentle Norfolk.

NORFOLK. I warrant you, my lord. [*Exit.*]

KING RICHARD III. Catesby!

CATESBY. My lord?

KING RICHARD III. Send out a pursuivant at arms
    To Stanley's regiment; bid him bring his power
    Before sun-rising, lest his son George fall
    Into the blind cave of eternal night.—[*Exit* CATESBY.]
    Fill me a bowl of wine.—Give me a watch.[281]—
    Saddle white Surrey for the field to-morrow.
    Look that my staves[282] be sound, and not too heavy.—
    Ratcliff,—

RATCLIFF. My lord?

KING RICHARD III. Saw'st thou the melancholy Lord Northumberland?

RATCLIFF. Thomas the Earl of Surrey, and himself,
    Much about cock-shut time,[283] from troop to troop
    Went through the army, cheering up the soldiers.

KING RICHARD III. So, I am satisfied.—Give me a bowl of wine:
    I have not that alacrity of spirit,
    Nor cheer of mind, that I was wont to have. [*Wine brought.*]
    Set it down.—Is ink and paper ready?

RATCLIFF. It is, my lord.

KING RICHARD III. Bid my guard watch; leave me.—Ratcliff,
    About the mid of night come to my tent
    And help to arm me.—Leave me, I say.

---

[280] The *beaver* was a part of the helmet fixed on a sort of hinge at the car, so as to be drawn down over the face or pushed up over the forehead, as the wearer chose or had occasion. It is probably in reference to this motion that *easier* is used of it.

[281] In calling for a *watch* Richard evidently does not mean a *sentinel*; for that guard should be kept about his tent was a matter of course. The *watch* called for is, no doubt, a *watch-light*, which was a night-candle so marked as to indicate how long it had burned, and thus serve the purpose of a modern *watch*.

[282] That is, the *staves* or poles of his lances. It was the custom to carry more than one into the field.

[283] A *cock-shut* was a large net stretched across a glade, and so suspended upon poles as easily to be drawn together, and was employed to catch woodcocks. These nets were chiefly used in the twilight of the evening, when woodcocks "take wing to go and get water, flying generally low; and when they find any thoroughfare, through a wood or range of trees, they venture through." The artificial glades made for them to pass through were called *cock*-roads. Hence *cock-shut time* and *cock-shut light* were used to express the evening twilight.

[*Exeunt* RATCLIFF *and the other Attendants.*]

[*Enter* STANLEY *to* RICHMOND *in his tent, Lords and others attending.*]

STANLEY. Fortune and victory sit on thy helm!
RICHMOND. All comfort that the dark night can afford
    Be to thy person, noble father-in-law!
    Tell me, how fares our loving mother?
STANLEY. I, by attorney, bless thee from thy mother
    Who prays continually for Richmond's good:
    So much for that.—The silent hours steal on,
    And flaky darkness breaks within the east.
    In brief,—for so the season bids us be,—
    Prepare thy battle early in the morning,
    And put thy fortune to the arbitrement
    Of bloody strokes and mortal-staring war.[284]
    I, as I may,—that which I would I cannot,—
    With best advantage will deceive the time,
    And aid thee in this doubtful shock of arms:
    But on thy side I may not be too forward
    Lest, being seen, thy brother, tender George,
    Be executed in his father's sight.
    Farewell: the leisure[285] and the fearful time
    Cuts off the ceremonious vows of love
    And ample interchange of sweet discourse,
    Which so long sunder'd friends should dwell upon:
    God give us leisure for these rites of love!
    Once more, adieu: be valiant, and speed well!
RICHMOND. Good lords, conduct him to his regiment:
    I'll strive, with troubled thoughts, to take a nap,
    Lest leaden slumber peise[286] me down to-morrow,
    When I should mount with wings of victory:
    Once more, good night, kind lords and gentlemen.

[*Exeunt* Officers, *&c., with* STANLEY.]

---

[284] "*Mortal staring* war" sounds rather odd and harsh, but probably means war looking with *deadly* eye, or staring *fatally*, on its victims. So the Poet very often uses *mortal* for that which *kills*, not that which *dies*.

[285] We still have a phrase equivalent to this, however harsh it may seem: "I would do this if *leisure* would permit"; where *leisure* stands for *want of leisure*. So in *King Richard II.*, i. 1: "Which then our *leisure would not let* us hear."

[286] *Peise* is an old form of *poise*, *weigh*; much used in the Poet's time.

O Thou, whose captain I account myself,
Look on my forces with a gracious eye;
Put in their hands thy bruising irons of wrath,
That they may crush down with a heavy fall
The usurping helmets of our adversaries!
Make us thy ministers of chastisement,
That we may praise thee in the victory!
To thee I do commend my watchful soul,
Ere I let fall the windows of mine eyes:
Sleeping and waking, O, defend me still! [*Sleeps.*]

[*Enter the Ghost of Prince* EDWARD, *son to King* HENRY *the Sixth, rises between the two tents.*]

GHOST of PRINCE. [*To* King RICHARD III.] Let me sit heavy on thy soul to-morrow!
Think, how thou stab'dst me in my prime of youth
At Tewksbury: despair, therefore, and die!—
[*To* RICHMOND.] Be cheerful, Richmond; for the wronged souls
Of butcher'd princes fight in thy behalf
King Henry's issue, Richmond, comforts thee.

[*The Ghost of King* HENRY *the Sixth rises.*]

GHOST of KING HENRY VI. [*To* King RICHARD III.] When I was mortal, my anointed body
By thee was punched full of deadly holes
Think on the Tower and me: despair, and die!
Harry the Sixth bids thee despair, and die!—
[*To* RICHMOND.] Virtuous and holy, be thou conqueror!
Harry, that prophesied thou shouldst be king,
Doth comfort thee in thy sleep: live, and flourish!

[*The Ghost of* CLARENCE *rises.*]

GHOST of CLARENCE. [*To* King RICHARD III.] Let me sit heavy on thy soul to-morrow!
I, that was wash'd to death with fulsome wine,[287]
Poor Clarence, by thy guile betrayed to death!
To-morrow in the battle think on me,
And fall thy edgeless sword: despair, and die!—

---

[287] *Fulsome* probably has reference to the qualities of Malmsey wine, which was peculiarly sweet and luscious, so much so as to cloy the appetite after a little drinking.— The Poet has represented Clarence as having been killed before he was thrown into the butt of wine. But one report gave it that he was drowned in such a cask of drink.

[*To* RICHMOND.] Thou offspring of the house of Lancaster
The wronged heirs of York do pray for thee
Good angels guard thy battle! live, and flourish!

[*The Ghosts of* RIVERS, GRAY, *and* VAUGHAN, *rise.*]

GHOST of RIVERS. [*To King* RICHARD III.] Let me sit heavy on thy soul to-
        morrow,
    Rivers. that died at Pomfret! despair, and die!
GHOST of GREY. [*To King* RICHARD III.] Think upon Grey, and let thy soul
        despair!
GHOST of VAUGHAN. [*To King* RICHARD III.] Think upon
        Vaughan, and, with guilty fear,
    Let fall thy lance: despair, and die!
ALL THREE. [*To* RICHMOND.] Awake, and think our wrongs in
Richard's bosom
    Will conquer him! awake, and win the day!

[*The Ghost of* HASTINGS *rises.*]

GHOST of HASTINGS. [*To King* RICHARD III.] Bloody and guilty,
        guiltily awake,
    And in a bloody battle end thy days!
    Think on Lord Hastings: despair, and die!
    [*To* RICHMOND.] Quiet untroubled soul, awake, awake!
    Arm, fight, and conquer, for fair England's sake!

[*The Ghosts of the two young* PRINCES *rise.*]

GHOSTS of YOUNG PRINCES. [*To* King RICHARD III.] Dream on
        thy cousins smother'd in the Tower:
    Let us be led within thy bosom, Richard,
    And weigh thee down to ruin, shame, and death!
    Thy nephews' souls bid thee despair and die!
    [*To* RICHMOND.] Sleep, Richmond, sleep in peace, and wake in
    joy;
    Good angels guard thee from the boar's annoy!
    Live, and beget a happy race of kings!
    Edward's unhappy sons do bid thee flourish.

[*The Ghost of* LADY ANNE *rises.*]

GHOST of LADY ANNE. [*To* KING RICHARD III.] Richard, thy
        wife, that wretched Anne thy wife,
    That never slept a quiet hour with thee,

Now fills thy sleep with perturbations
To-morrow in the battle think on me,
And fall thy edgeless sword: despair, and die!—
[*To* RICHMOND.] Thou quiet soul, sleep thou a quiet sleep
Dream of success and happy victory!
Thy adversary's wife doth pray for thee.

[*The Ghost of* BUCKINGHAM *rises.*]

GHOST of BUCKINGHAM. [*To* King RICHARD III.] The last was I
    that helped thee to the crown;
The last was I that felt thy tyranny:
O, in the battle think on Buckingham,
And die in terror of thy guiltiness!
Dream on, dream on, of bloody deeds and death:
Fainting, despair; despairing, yield thy breath!
[*To* RICHMOND.] I died for hope[288] ere I could lend thee aid:
But cheer thy heart, and be thou not dismay'd:
God and good angel fight on Richmond's side!
And Richard falls in height of all his pride![289]

[*The Ghosts vanish. King* RICHARD III *starts out of his dream.*]

KING RICHARD III. Give me another horse,—bind up my wounds,—
Have mercy, Jesu!—Soft! I did but dream.—
O coward conscience, how dost thou afflict me!—
The lights burn blue.—It is now dead midnight.
Cold fearful drops stand on my trembling flesh.
What do I fear? myself? there's none else by:
Richard loves Richard; that is, I am I.
Is there a murderer here? No;—yes, I am:
Then fly. What, from myself? Great reason why,—
Lest I revenge. What, myself upon myself?
Alack. I love myself. Wherefore? for any good
That I myself have done unto myself?

---

[288] Buckingham's *hope* of aiding Richmond induced him to take up arms: he lost his life in consequence, and therefore may be said to have died *for* hope; hope being the *cause* which led to that event.

[289] In this series of speeches the Poet has with happy effect given a "local habitation and a name" to what is thus stated in the *Chronicles*: "The fame went, that he had the same night a terrible dreame; for it seemed to him, being asleepe, that he did see diverse images like terrible divels, which pulled and haled him, not suffering him to take anie quiet or rest. The which strange vision not so suddenlie strake his heart with feare, but it stuffed his head with many busie and dreadfull imaginations. For incontinent after, his heart being almost damped, he prognosticated the doubtfull chance of the battle, not using the alacritie and mirth of mind and countenance as he was accustomed to doo."

O, no! alas, I rather hate myself
For hateful deeds committed by myself!
I am a villain: yet I lie. I am not.
Fool, of thyself speak well:—fool, do not flatter.
My conscience hath a thousand several tongues,
And every tongue brings in a several tale,
And every tale condemns me for a villain.
Perjury, perjury, in the high'st degree
Murder, stem murder, in the direst degree;
All several sins, all used in each degree,
Throng to the bar, crying all, *Guilty! guilty!*
I shall despair. There is no creature loves me;
And if I die, no soul shall pity me:
Nay, wherefore should they, since that I myself
Find in myself no pity to myself?[290]

[*Re-enter* RATCLIFF.]

RATCLIFF. My lord!
KING RICHARD III. 'Zounds! who is there?
RATCLIFF. Ratcliff, my lord; 'tis I. The early village-cock
Hath twice done salutation to the morn;
Your friends are up, and buckle on their armour.
KING RICHARD III. O Ratcliff, I have dream'd a fearful dream!
What thinkest thou, will our friends prove all true?
RATCLIFF. No doubt, my lord.
KING RICHARD III. O Ratcliff, I fear, I fear,—
RATCLIFF. Nay, good my lord, be not afraid of shadows.
KING RICHARD III. By the apostle Paul, shadows to-night
Have struck more terror to the soul of Richard
Than can the substance of ten thousand soldiers
Armed in proof[291] and led by shallow Richmond.
It is not yet near day. Come, go with me;
Under our tents I'll play the eaves-dropper,
To see if any mean to shrink from me.

[*Exeunt King* RICHARD III *and* RATCLIFF.]

[*Re-enter* OXFORD, *with other Lords, &c.*]

---

[290] In this strange speech there are some ten lines in or near the Poet's best style; the others are in his worst; so inferior indeed, that it is not easy to understand how Shakespeare could have written them at all.

[291] "Armed in *proof*" is encased in armour that is proof against warlike weapons. Probably the phrase is meant to include offensive as well as defensive armour.

LORDS. Good morrow, Richmond!

RICHMOND. [*Waking.*] Cry mercy, lords and watchful gentlemen,
That you have ta'en a tardy sluggard here.

LORDS. How have you slept, my lord?

RICHMOND. The sweetest sleep, and fairest-boding dreams
That ever enter'd in a drowsy head,
Have I since your departure had, my lords.
Methought their souls, whose bodies Richard murder'd,
Came to my tent, and cried, *On! victory!*
I promise you, my soul is very jocund
In the remembrance of so fair a dream.
How far into the morning is it, lords?

LORDS. Upon the stroke of four.

RICHMOND. Why, then 'tis time to arm and give direction.—

[*He advances to the Troops.*]

More than I have said, loving countrymen,
The leisure[292] and enforcement of the time
Forbids to dwell upon: yet remember this,
God and our good cause fight upon our side;
The prayers of holy saints and wronged souls,
Like high-rear'd bulwarks, stand before our faces;
Richard except, those whom we fight against
Had rather have us win than him they follow:
For what is he they follow? truly, gentlemen,
A bloody tyrant and a homicide;
One raised in blood, and one in blood establish'd;
One that made means to come by what he hath,
And slaughter'd those that were the means to help him;
Abase foul stone, made precious by the foil
Of England's chair, where he is falsely set;[293]
One that hath ever been God's enemy:
Then, if you fight against God's enemy,
God will in justice ward you as his soldiers;
If you do sweat to put a tyrant down,
You sleep in peace, the tyrant being slain;
If you do fight against your country's foes,
Your country's fat shall pay your pains the hire;
If you do fight in safeguard of your wives,
Your wives shall welcome home the conquerors;

---

[292] *Leisure*, again, for *want of leisure*. See page 122, note 285.

[293] "England's *chair*" is the *throne*. The allusion is to the practice of setting gems of little worth, with a bright-coloured *foil* under them.

> If you do free your children from the sword,
> Your children's children quit[294] it in your age.
> Then, in the name of God and all these rights,
> Advance your standards, draw your willing swords.
> For me, the ransom of my bold attempt
> Shall be this cold corpse on the earth's cold face;
> But if I thrive, the gain of my attempt
> The least of you shall share his part thereof.—
> Sound drums and trumpets boldly and cheerfully;
> God and Saint George! Richmond and victory! [*Exeunt.*]

[*Re-enter King* RICHARD, RATCLIFF, *Attendants and Forces.*]

KING RICHARD III. What said Northumberland as touching
    Richmond?
RATCLIFF. That he was never trained up in arms.
KING RICHARD III. He said the truth: and what said Surrey then?
RATCLIFF. He smiled and said, *The better for our purpose.*
KING RICHARD III. He was in the right; and so indeed it is.—

    [*Clock strikes.*]

> Tell the clock there.—Give me a calendar.—
> Who saw the sun to-day?
RATCLIFF. Not I, my lord.
KING RICHARD III. Then he disdains to shine; for by the book
    He should have braved[295] the east an hour ago
    A black day will it be to somebody.—
    Ratcliff,—
RATCLIFF. My lord?
KING RICHARD III. The sun will not be seen to-day;
    The sky doth frown and lour upon our army.
    I would these dewy tears were from the ground.
    Not shine to-day! Why, what is that to me
    More than to Richmond? for the selfsame heaven
    That frowns on me looks sadly upon him.

    [*Enter* NORFOLK.]

NORFOLK. Arm, arm, my lord; the foe vaunts in the field.
KING RICHARD III. Come, bustle, bustle;—caparison my horse;—
    Call up Lord Stanley, bid him bring his power:

---

[294] *Quit*, again, in the sense of *requite*. See page 100, note 223.
[295] To *brave* is, in one of its senses, to *make fine*, *splendid*, or *glorious*.

I will lead forth my soldiers to the plain,
And thus my battle shall be ordered:
My forward shall be drawn out all in length,
Consisting equally of horse and foot;
Our archers shall be placed in the midst
John Duke of Norfolk, Thomas Earl of Surrey,
Shall have the leading of this foot and horse.
They thus directed, we will follow
In the main battle, whose puissance on either side
Shall be well winged with our chiefest horse.
This, and Saint George to boot![296]—What think'st thou, Norfolk?
NORFOLK. A good direction, warlike sovereign.
This found I on my tent this morning. [Giving a scroll.]
KING RICHARD III. [Reads.] Jockey of Norfolk, be not too bold,
For Dickon thy master is bought and sold.[297]
A thing devised by the enemy.
Go, gentleman, every man unto his charge
Let not our babbling dreams affright our souls:
Conscience is but a word that cowards use,
Devised at first to keep the strong in awe:
Our strong arms be our conscience, swords our law.
March on, join bravely, let us to't pell-mell
If not to Heaven, then hand in hand to Hell.—
[To his Soldiers.] What shall I say more than I have inferr'd?[298]
Remember whom you are to cope withal;
A sort[299] of vagabonds, rascals, and runaways,
A scum of Bretons, and base lackey peasants,
Whom their o'er-cloyed country vomits forth
To desperate ventures and assured destruction.
You sleeping safe, they bring to you unrest;
You having lands, and blest with beauteous wives,

---

[296] This, and Saint George to help us, into the bargain.

[297] So in the *Chronicles*: "John duke of Norffolke was warned by diverse to refrain from the field, insomuch that the night before he should set forward toward the king, one wrote this rime upon his gate:

> Jocke of Norffolke, be not too bold,
> For Dickon thy maister is bought and sold."

Jocky and *Dickon* were familiar forms of *John* and *Richard*.—*Bought and sold* was a sort of proverbial phrase for *hopelessly ruined by treacherous practices*.

[298] Here again we have *inferr'd* for *brought forward* or *alleged*.

[299] *Sort* here means *crew, pack*, or *set*. So in *2 Henry VI.*, iii. 2: "He was the lord ambassador sent from a sort of tinkers to the King." And in *A Midsummer-Night's Dream*, iii. 2, Puck describes Bottom as "the shallowest thickskin of that barren *sort*"; referring to the "crew of patches" who are getting up the interlude of *Pyramus* and *Thisbe*.

They would distrain[300] the one, distain the other.
And who doth lead them but a paltry fellow,
Long kept in Bretagne at our mother's cost?[301]
A milk-sop, one that never in his life
Felt so much cold as over shoes in snow?
Let's whip these stragglers o'er the seas again;
Lash hence these overweening rags of France,
These famish'd beggars, weary of their lives;
Who, but for dreaming on this fond exploit,
For want of means, poor rats, had hang'd themselves:
If we be conquer'd, let men conquer us,
And not these bastard Bretons; whom our fathers
Have in their own land beaten, bobb'd, and thump'd,
And in record, left them the heirs of shame.
Shall these enjoy our lands? lie with our wives?
Ravish our daughters? [*Drum afar off.*] Hark! I hear their drum.—
Fight, gentlemen of England! fight, bold yoemen!
Draw, archers, draw your arrows to the head!
Spur your proud horses hard, and ride in blood;
Amaze the welkin with your broken staves![302]—

[*Enter a* MESSENGER.]

What says Lord Stanley? will he bring his power?
Messenger. My lord, he doth deny to come.
KING RICHARD III. Off with his son George's head!
NORFOLK. My lord, the enemy is past the marsh:[303]
    After the battle let George Stanley die.
KING RICHARD III. A thousand hearts are great within my bosom:
    Advance our standards, set upon our foes
    Our ancient word of courage, fair Saint George,

---

[300] *Distrain* is here used in its old sense of *lawless seizure.*

[301] This should be "at our *brother's* cost." Richmond was in fact held in a sort of honourable custody at the Duke of Bretagne's Court, his means being supplied by Charles, Duke of Burgundy, who was Richard's brotherin-law. Hall gives the matter thus: "And to begyn with the earle of Richmond Captaine of this rebellion, he is a Welsh mylkesoppe, a man of small courage, and of lesse experience in marcyall acts and feates of warr, brought up by my brothers meanes and myne like a captive in a close cage in the court of Frances duke of Britaine." Holinshed copied Hall's account, but in Holinshed's second edition "*moothers* meanes" got misprinted for "*brothers* meunes"; and hence the Poet's mistake.

[302] Fright the skies with the shivers of your lances.

[303] Betweene both armies there was a great marish, which the earle of Richmond left on his right hand; for this intent, that it should be on that side a defense for his part, and in so dooing he had the sunne at his backe, and in the faces of his enimies. When king Richard saw the earles companie was passed the marish, he did command with all hast to set upon them.—HOLINSHED.

Inspire us with the spleen of fiery dragons!
Upon them! victory sits on our helms. [*Exeunt.*]

SCENE IV.

Another Part of the Field.

[*Alarums*: *excursions. Enter* NORFOLK *and Forces*; *to him*
CATESBY.]

CATESBY. Rescue, my Lord of Norfolk, rescue, rescue!
The king enacts more wonders than a man,
Daring an opposite to every danger:[304]
His horse is slain, and all on foot he fights,
Seeking for Richmond in the throat of death.
Rescue, fair lord, or else the day is lost!

[*Alarums. Enter King* RICHARD III.]

KING RICHARD III. A horse! a horse! my kingdom for a horse!
CATESBY. Withdraw, my lord; I'll help you to a horse.
KING RICHARD III. Slave, I have set my life upon a cast,
And I will stand the hazard of the die:
I think there be six Richmonds in the field;
Five have I slain to-day instead of him.[305]—
A horse! a horse! my kingdom for a horse! [*Exeunt.*]

---

[304] The Poet repeatedly uses *opposite* for *opponent* or *adversary*. So that "daring an opposite to every danger" probably means *offering himself as an opponent* in every danger, or, which comes to the same thing, challenging every dangerous antagonist to fight with him.

[305] Shakespeare employs this incident with historical propriety in The First Part of *King Henry IV*. He had here also good ground for his poetical exaggeration. Richard, according to the *Chronicles*, was determined if possible to engage with Richmond in single combat. For this purpose he rode furiously to that quarter of the field where the Earl was; attacked his standard bearer, Sir William Brandon, and killed him; then assaulted Sir John Cheney, whom he overthrew. Having thus at length cleared his way to his antagonist, he engaged in single combat with him, and probably would have been victorious, but that at that instant Sir William Stanley with three thousand men joined Richmond's army, and the royal forces fled with great precipitation. Richard was soon afterwards overpowered by numbers, and fell, fighting bravely to the last.

SCENE V.

Another Part of the Field.

[*Alarums. Enter, from opposite sides, King* RICHARD III *and* RICHMOND; *they fight, and exeunt fighting. Retreat and flourish. Then re-enter* RICHMOND, STANLEY *bearing the crown, with divers other* Lords, *and Forces.*]

RICHMOND. God and your arms be praised, victorious friends,
    The day is ours, the bloody dog is dead.
STANLEY. Courageous Richmond, well hast thou acquit[306] thee.
    Lo, here, this long-usurped royalty
    From the dead temples of this bloody wretch
    Have I pluck'd off, to grace thy brows withal:
    Wear it, enjoy it, and make much of it.
RICHMOND. Great God of heaven, say Amen to all!—
    But, tell me, is young George Stanley living?
STANLEY. He is, my lord, and safe in Leicester town;
    Whither, if it please you, we may now withdraw us.
RICHMOND. What men of name are slain on either side?
STANLEY. John Duke of Norfolk, Walter Lord Ferrers,
    Sir Robert Brakenbury, and Sir William Brandon.
RICHMOND. Inter their bodies as becomes their births:
    Proclaim a pardon to the soldiers fled
    That in submission will return to us:
    And then, as we have ta'en the sacrament,
    We will unite the white rose and the red:—
    Smile heaven upon this fair conjunction,
    That long have frown'd upon their enmity!—
    What traitor hears me, and says not amen?
    England hath long been mad, and scarr'd herself;
    The brother blindly shed the brother's blood,
    The father rashly slaughter'd his own son,
    The son, compell'd, been butcher to the sire:
    All this divided York and Lancaster,
    Divided in their dire division,
    O, now, let Richmond and Elizabeth,
    The true succeeders of each royal House,—
    Divided in their dire division.—
    By God's fair ordinance conjoin together!
    And let their heirs—God, if thy will be so—

---

[306] *Acquit* for *acquitted.* See page 47, note 90, and page 74, note 149.

Enrich the time to come with smooth-faced peace,
With smiling plenty and fair prosperous days!
Abate[307] the edge of traitors, gracious Lord,
That would reduce[308] these bloody days again,
And make poor England weep in streams of blood!
Let them not live to taste this land's increase
That would with treason wound this fair land's peace!
Now civil wounds are stopp'd, peace lives again:
That she may long live here, God say amen! [*Exeunt.*]

THE END

---

[307] *Abate* here means *make dull*, like *rebate*. So, in *Love's Labours Lost*, i. 1: "That honour which shall '*bate* his scythe's keen edge." Also, in the novel of *Pericles*, 1608: "Absence *abates* that edge that presence whets." And Florio: "Spontare,—to *abate the edge or point of any thing or weapon, to blunt, to unpoint.*"

[308] *Reduce*, again, in the Latin sense of *bring back*. See page 56, note 108.

34781921R00080